Odyssey
with the Goddess

Snake Goddess found at Kato Chorio, near Ierapetra, Crete

ODYSSEY
with the
GODDESS

---

*A Spiritual Quest
in Crete*

CAROL P. CHRIST

CONTINUUM • NEW YORK

1995
The Continuum Publishing Company
370 Lexington Avenue, New York, NY 10017

Printed in the United States of America

Library of Congress Cataloging-in-Publication Data

Christ, Carol P.
    Odyssey with the goddess : a spiritual quest in Crete / Carol P.
Christ
        p.   cm.
    Includes bibliographical references.
    ISBN 0-8264-0793-5 (hbk. : alk paper)
    1. Christ, Carol P. 2. Spiritual biography—United States.
3. Goddess religion. 4. Crete—Description and travel. 5. Crete—
Religion. I. Travel
BL73.C395A3 1995
291.2'082—dc20   94-47965
    [B]   CIP

Map of Crete designed by Dale Hasenick.

this book is dedicated to F. T.
who offered love in time of death

to my two adopted sisters
Naomi Goldenberg and Jana Ruble
who were with me in Crete

to Mara Keller and Carol Wilken
whose prodding got me to Crete

to Charis Kataki and Patrick Thomassin
who helped me to see and to trust

to Melpo Troumbi
who was with me as we probed
the darkness within

and to Nikos Belias
brother in spirit
who approached the gates of death
and turned back

Untranslated hieroglyphic writing of the Phaistos Disk

Two steps left
Two steps right
Into the darkness
Into the light

CONTENTS

List of Illustrations   xi
Acknowledgments   xiii
Preface   1

Part One · *Underworld*
Disappointment   9
Death   18
Grief   24

Part Two · *Rebirth*
The Sacred Myrtle Tree   33
Mysteries   36
Reluctant Guests at the Dionysian Rites   39
Challenge   43
Trusting the Dark   45
Flowers of Spring   48
Gifts   50
Promise   52
Surprise   54
Revelation   55
Words with You, Aphrodite   59
Everyone Is Waiting for You to Come Back   61
Forgiveness   64
On the Far Side of Death   66
Thanksgiving   69

On the Far Side of Death   66
Thanksgiving   69

Part Three · *Pilgrimage*
Preparation   77
Everything Under Control   80
Help Abounding   83
Language of the Goddess   85
Rituals at Knossos   88
The Tree of Life   92
Taste the Sweetness   95
Music in Zaros   98
Beginning Here   100
Surpassing Every Expectation   104
Harvest Home   110
Panagia in Chains   113
Sour Milk   115
Amazing Grace   118
I Once Was Lost   120
But Now I'm Found   123
The Dance Is About to Begin   125
Mochlos Mother   129
A Difficult Passage   134
Many Blessings   137
A Brilliant Suggestion   142
Giveaway   144
Mountain Women   148
Minoan Sisterhood   151

Part Four · *Revelations*
Incubation   159
Insight   161
A Serpentine Path   163

Notes   *169*

LIST OF ILLUSTRATIONS

Snake Goddess found at Kato Chorio, near Ierapetra, Crete. Burnished terra cotta, Neolithic, c. 6500–3500 B.C.E. Heraklion Museum.   ii

Untranslated hiroglyphic writing of the Phaistos Disk, found in the treasury of the old palace at Phaistos, Crete. Terra cotta, Minoan, c. 1700 B.C.E. Heraklion Museum.   vi

Map of Crete.   xiv–xv

Woman pouring an offering to the dead onto an altar flanked by two double axes with birds (epiphanies of the Goddess) perched on top of them. Detail of a fresco on a stone sarcophagus found in a tomb at Agia Triada, Crete, post-Minoan, c. 1400 B.C.E. Heraklion Museum.   4

The miracle-working Panagia of Palianí with silver hands. Palianí convent near Venerato, Crete.   28

Women dancing in a meadow with lilies, Goddess descending from the sky, snakes, an eye, a chrysalis, and a shoot in the background. Gold ring found in the tomb at Isopata near Knossos, Crete, Minoan, c. 1500 B.C.E. Heraklion Museum.   72

Efsevia Sylignaki of Skaka, Crete.   132

Snake Goddesses from Knossos in Minoan ritual costume. Faience, found in the treasury of the new palace at Knossos, Crete, Minoan, c. 1600 B.C.E. Heraklion Museum.   154

Women dancing in a circle to the music of a lyre player. Terra cotta, found at Palaikastro, Crete, post-Minoan, c. 1400–1100 B.C.E. Heraklion Museum.   166

ACKNOWLEDGMENTS

$\mathcal{A}$s always, my editor Marie Cantlon was a sensitive and enthusiastic reader. Frank Oveis recognized this book's potential and helped to bring it to a speedy completion. Martha Ann, Ellen Boneparth, Karin Carrington, Christine Downing, Patricia Felch, Jennifer Freed, Naomi Goldenberg, Leila Kourayianni, Liz Lerner, River Malcolm, Judith Plaskow, Jana Ruble, Tina Salowey, Judy Shavrien, Jill Singer, Melpo Troumbi, and Pamela Westfall-Rosen provided helpful readings of all or parts of the manuscript. Judith Shaw created the collage, "Twentieth Century Snake Goddess," that is the cover illustration.

The photographs of Cretan artifacts were supplied by Ekdotike Athenon, S.A.; permission to publish them was granted by the Heraklion Museum. The photograph of Efsevia Sylignaki was a gift from her family. The photograph of the Panagia of Paliani is reproduced with the permission of the nuns of Paliani. The quotations from Sappho are reprinted with permission from Mary Barnard, translator, *Sappho: A New Translation*, University of California Press. Copyright © 1958, 1986 Mary Barnard.

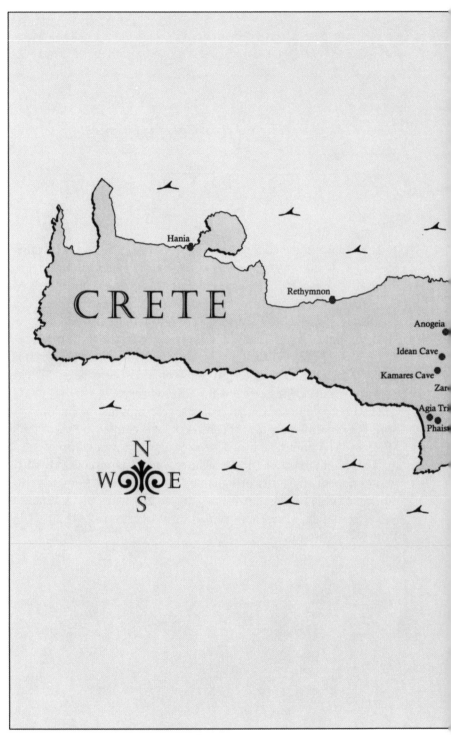

CRETE

Hania

Rethymnon

Anogeia

Idean Cave

Kamares Cave

Zar

Agia Tri

Phaist

N
W   E
S

Map of Crete

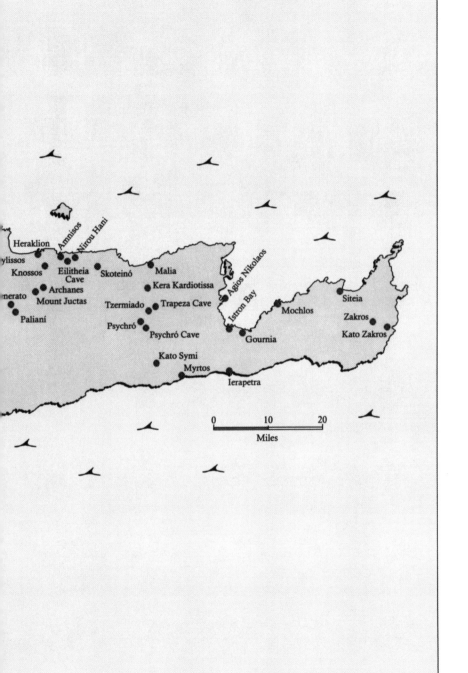

Heraklion
Amnisos
Nirou Hani
ylissos
Knossos
Eilitheia
Cave
Skoteinó
Malia
Kera Kardiotissa
Archanes
erato
Mount Juctas
Tzermiado
Trapeza Cave
Agios Nikolaos
Istron Bay
Siteia
Mochlos
Paliɑní
Psychró
Psychró Cave
Gournia
Zakros
Kato Zakros
Kato Symi
Myrtos
Ierapetra

0   10   20
Miles

PREFACE

$\mathscr{B}$ecause this book, like much writing by women, breaks the boundaries of genre, it is appropriate to say a few words about its purpose at the outset.

As many spiritual teachers have understood, the meaning of life cannot be reduced to a few simple words, nor can it be encompassed in theory, philosophy, or theology. The meaning of life, embedded in story and symbol, can be understood only through living. Each of my acadamic interests—from my studies of the poetry of the prophets, to my work on the narrative theology of Elie Wiesel, to my analysis of the theme of women's spiritual quest in the poetry and prose of contemporary women, to my attempts to integrate thealogy and experience in my own work—has reflected my interest in forms of religious expression that are connected to experience.

In contrast, the academic communities in which I worked and studied—including the feminist ones—have for the most part valued theory over embodied knowing. For me, theory alone has become a dead end. For example, it has been stated and stated again in feminist thealogies that the Goddess represents birth, death, and rebirth; the acceptance and affirmation of change. But what does this really mean? Is it so easy for a woman or man who has grown up in a control-oriented culture to integrate this idea into life? I have written about accepting finitude and change many times without realizing that I was very far from living the ideas I espoused. In order to bridge the gap between theory and experience, I have turned to story.

Odyssey with the Goddess depicts a spiritual journey from death and despair to healing and rebirth. At its deepest level, it is a story with universal resonance. It is also a woman's story, a spiritual quest told from a particular point of view.

The story begins with a very female experience of despair—abandonment in a love relationship. What follows is a journey not willingly or consciously chosen. At its outset, the protagonist is required to be present as her mother dies. In the process, she glimpses the mystery of love but is not yet ready to incorporate its meaning into her life.

She is taken to Crete, a land where the Goddess once reigned in peace and harmony. There she descends into the darkness of a cave, sensing a very female mystery, finds the tree of life in the center of the garden, and dances to the strange rhythms of mountain goat songs. Strengthened by these experiences, she can begin to confront the source of her despair.

On her return to Crete, circumstances conspire to force her to give up the illusion that she is in control. As she succumbs to exhaustion and illness, and accepts the help that is offered along the way, she experiences another way of living. She understands that the father's message of self-control that has shaped her life leads to despair and death. She learns to replace self-control with vulnerability to human emotion and openness to the manifold manifestations of love; despair with the sure and certain knowledge that we are never alone in life or death. She understands that life is not a goal to be achieved by effort and will, but rather is a dance along a serpentine path offering many gifts at every turn.

Odyssey with the Goddess is a narrative thealogy, the story of my quest to understand my relation to the ground of being, to the power or powers that sustain my life and all life, and to name divinity out of the depths of my experience. My journey is guided at every point by the Goddess. Present in the rocks that undergird life, in the darkness where life is conceived and transformed, in the air and the everchanging waters, the Goddess is the love that supports embodied and relational being. Does this mean that the divinity cannot also be named and invoked with male names and symbols? Of course not. But in this story—and in the lives of many women—it is She who appears.

As Augustine's *Confessions* helped others to comprehend the role the new Christian God could play in men's lives, this story, written at the beginning of another age, helps us to understand the strength a contemporary woman can gain through her relation to the Goddess. Augustine's telling of the Christian story was incomplete, describing the journey only from one man's point of view. So too, this story is incomplete, reminding us that we each need to tell our stories as we discover new ways of understanding and naming the meanings of our lives.

Part One

UNDERWORLD

Woman pouring an offering to the dead onto an altar flanked by two large double axes with birds (epiphanies of the Goddess) perched on top of them

. . . while I . . . cut a trench a cubit long
and a cubit broad. Round it, I poured
a libation to all the dead, first with
milk and honey, then with sweet wine,
then with water . . .

· Homer, reporting customs that no
doubt were ancient in his time

⌇⌇⌇ When I left the United States and moved to Lesbos, I felt called by the Goddess to live more fully from my heart and through my body. My intuition that I would learn a different way of living in Greece was not wrong, but I would have to give up more than an academic position in order to learn the lesson Greece had to teach.

Shortly after I settled in Greece, matters came to a crisis point: I would have to face my demons and uproot my most deeply held, only partially conscious, assumptions about life, or continue to live with anger, despair, and bitterness, cut off from the source of creativity and joy.

Though it may have seemed that I was marking time while I furnished my home and learned to cook, I was connecting to a repressed female part of myself, the love of beauty and delight in nurturing that had been my mother's and grandmother's legacies to me.

My mother's dying forced me to acknowledge the depth of my love for her and to recognize the bond we shared, despite the separations caused by my mother's deference to my father and my brothers, and by my decision to honor the fathers by putting career before marriage and family.

Reconnecting with my mother at the time of her death opened my heart and enabled me to sense a great mystery, the mystery of love.

DISAPPOINTMENT

Last night

I dreamed that
you and I had
words: Cyprian.[1]

ore than two and a half thousand years ago, the poet Sappho was bold enough to express her anger at the Goddess Aphrodite. I too had been having words with Aphrodite. Or more precisely, holding onto an enormous anger that precluded words. I no longer prayed to the Goddess who had inspired me to hope that eros and ecstasy could be mine. Even worse, I no longer trusted my deepest feelings and intuitions, the source not only of my relationship to the Goddess, but also of my creativity. It had become a struggle for me just to live, to suppress the words that came unbidden into my mind, threatening to blot out all else: "*No one understands me, no one loves me, no one will ever love me, I might as well die.*" I believed I had a right to be angry with the Goddess because my devotion to her had brought me to live in Sappho's land and, in a deeper sense, to the impasse where I found myself.

I had first come to Greece, reluctantly, ten years earlier. My friend Ellen, who had fallen in love with Greece, organized a summer institute in Lesbos and insisted that I teach the course on Greek Goddesses. Though I had been seeking the Goddess for many years, the Greek Goddesses were not in my blood. I was not one of those girls whose mothers had read them bedtime stories of the Greek Goddesses and Gods. Nor had I found books about Greek mythology in the library or learned about it in school. In college, my passion had been devoted to the study of the Hebrew Bible. Because I knew more about the culture in which they were rooted, it was natural that I would feel more drawn to the Hebrew Goddesses—Astarte naked, holding flowers, or Asherah, with a body like a tree trunk—than to the less-familiar and less immediately attractive warlike Athena or jealous and vindictive Hera. Because I understood the Goddesses to be embodied in nature, I felt called to learn about the Grandmothers of the American land where I lived. But Ellen, who usually gets what she wants, would not take no for an answer. So, in the late spring of 1981, I packed my bags and traveled to Lesbos, where I would learn and teach about the Greek Goddesses. I did not know that one summer would soon become five, nor that, in time, I would come to feel more at home in Greece than anywhere else.

Lesbos is a large island with surviving pine forests on a central mountain range. Silvery green olive trees dot the hillsides. The island embraces the wide Gulf of Kalloni, "the beautiful," in its center. Mythimna, the village where we stayed, is at the island's northernmost end, in sight of the shores of Turkey. Achilles is said to have plundered Mythimna during lulls in the Trojan War. Grey stone houses with gaily colored shutters and terra-cotta roofs climb the sides of a hill that is topped by an austere brown stone fortress built by Genoese warlords on foundations dating at least to Byzantine times. It was last occupied by the Turks who lost control of Lesbos in 1912 but did not leave the island until after the defeat of the Greek army in Asia Minor in 1922. Turkish words still embellish the many dialects of the villages.

Lesbos was home to Sappho, Greece's most honored lyric poet, whom Plato called "the tenth muse." The muses still sing in Lesbos, in the tinkling of sheep's bells and in the plaintive calls of the doves. A local story, told to me by my first Greek friend, the beautiful Axiothea, says that the dove was once a young girl who lost her love. The dove's cry, *deka-octo*, *deka-octo*, sounding like the Greek word for eighteen, is her repetition of her sweetheart's age when he died.

The deep bay of Mythimna is sheltered by the hills of Petra on one side and a tiny fishing harbor on the other. Its waters are placid, but ever-moving currents reflect the light in colors ranging from grey, to blue, to indigo. The crystal-clear light unique to Greece is often pierced by the graceful swoops and dives of swallows who make their mud nests on the sides of the houses. One can swim out a long, long way, all the while looking up at the village, without reaching the open sea. At sunset, the black silhouettes of fishing boats crisscross the horizon as the evening star rises in the wake of the setting sun.

Though the Goddess is present in the landscape of Lesbos, there are no impressive ruins of ancient temples. In a place called Mesa, a few grey stones and broken columns in the marshy place where sea meets dry land mark the site of a Hellenistic temple to Aphrodite.[2] When the women from the institute first visited the site, we found it unfenced, with two trees growing in its center and a spring gurgling nearby. The local farmers and their animals moved slowly in the summer heat. A heavy calm seemed to descend upon us. We poured water from a ceramic pitcher into the welcoming earth, and read to each other from the poems of Sappho. It was not difficult to imagine that Sappho and her students had also visited this sacred place.

The next summer a friend and I made a pilgrimage to the temple together, to heal the pain of broken love. As we crossed the temple's threshhold, an unexpected golden laughter filled the air.[3] The laughter of Aphrodite seemed to be urging me not to take my suffering so seriously. Later, sitting alone between the trees, I felt the warm sun transform the pain I held in my body. I knew I was being claimed by the Goddess, but I had no inkling that my initiation was the beginning of an odyssey that would require me to leave behind home and family, work and dear friends, and move to a foreign land.[4]

The Aphrodite I discovered on my pilgrimages to her temple and through study was not the superficial Goddess of sexuality, love, and beauty portrayed in the myths of Homer and Hesiod. I learned to look beyond Homer and Hesiod, who, like the authors of the Bible, were motivated by "the ugly malice of theological animus."[5] Their goal was to disempower the Goddesses in order to establish the hegemony of the Father of all the Gods, Zeus. To understand Aphrodite, we must return to Her source. Like all the Goddesses, Aphrodite rose from the Earth. Sexuality, love, and beauty are the creative powers of the Earth as mother of all: sexuality stimulates the cycles of birth and rebirth; love supports and sustains life; beauty is a great gift of bounteous Earth. To reclaim *this* Aphrodite is to acknowledge that we too are rooted in the Earth.

In the ensuing years, I taught about Aphrodite, wrote about her, tended her shrines, performed her rituals, and brought many women and girls to be initiated at her temple.[6] When I was teaching and lecturing in the summer program on Sappho's isle, others frequently said that I seemed to embody the Goddess Aphrodite for them. Swimming in the grey blue sea in Mythimna, I felt alive, whole, at peace.

When I returned to California each fall, I tried to infuse the energy I had contacted in Lesbos into my teaching and daily life. But with freeway driving bringing me to school, students taking my courses to fulfill requirements, ugly classrooms, bells marking the beginning and ending of our time together, the stress of deadlines and grading, and an institutional structure that favored objective tests over the more subtle measures of real learning, I usually felt exhausted and deadened midway into the semester.

The powers associated with Aphrodite as a particular manifestation of the Goddess—eros and ecstasy, intuition and deep feeling, the life force in nature and our bodies—were also for me a muse, opening me to a more poetic, more rhythmic, and more grounded style of writing. The essay I wrote for a panel on "Initiation" in the Women and Religion section of the American Academy of Religion was a decisive turning point in my career.[7] For this session, I was asked to reflect on how the impact of my "initiation" into a nontraditional form of spirituality had affected my work in religious studies. Writing this essay forced me to bring together two strands in my work: my experience of the Goddess and my theoretical work. Participating in the panel was a catalyst that led me to combine stories about my personal journey with thealogical reflection in my book *Laughter of Aphrodite*. My work was moving in the direction of the kind of embodied thinking I had struggled to define in *Diving Deep and Surfacing*, my earlier work on religion and literature, narrative theology, and women's spiritual quest.[8] Previously, I had written about how spirituality emerges in the stories we tell about our lives through analysis of the works of others. Now I was starting to write my own narrative thealogy, in which my understanding of the Goddess emerged in the telling of the stories of *my* life. I was discovering my authentic voice.

Not surprisingly, as I came more in touch with my deepest feelings and began to express them in my writing, my work began to move farther away from accepted academic models. My dream of one day being offered a more satisfying academic postion began to seem less and less likely. Ironically (and painfully), as the Goddess became central in my work, I also began to feel isolated in the place that had previously felt like my academic home: the Women and Religion section of the American Academy of Religion. The academy was neither training nor rewarding women to study ancient and modern Goddess religions; those of us who chose to do so in an academic setting found our voices drowned out by an increasingly moralistic chorus of Christian feminists, whose dialogue was with each other, not with women who had left the church.

In the summers, when I returned to Lesbos, the Goddess seemed to call me to come closer to Her. In time, I allowed Aphrodite's power to penetrate my bones, to transform my soul so fully that I could no longer return each fall to a culture that sapped the life energy I felt so strongly in Greece. Under the influence of the Goddess, I took leaves of absence from my job and moved to Lesbos, first for four months, and then for a year. Walking the cobbled steps to my house at the top of the hill, looking down across tiled roofs to the sea below, I knew I would stay. Six years after I first came to Lesbos, five years after my initiation at Aphrodite's temple, my marriage ended. I resigned the tenured full professorship I had worked so hard to achieve. Greece had become my home. I never for one moment looked back.

When I moved to Lesbos, I was warmly greeted by the many Greek friends I had made over the years. Axiothea, the first woman to open her own shop in Mythimna; her mother Ellie, whose marriage had been arranged when she was fifteen and who described herself as a feminist; and Nena, who remembered the first summer the group spent in Lesbos as the happiest time in her life, were my closest friends. Whenever I knocked on their doors, they stopped what they were doing and made Turkish coffee that we drank out of small cups while sharing the stories of our lives in broken Greek and English. Afterwards, we often read our fortunes in the coffee cups.

By lucky chance, another American woman, Jude, an artist with long brown hair and a direct, earthy way of speaking and moving, had come to live in Lesbos about the same time I did. Together we shared the struggles of adjusting to a foreign culture and talked about how the beauty of the land and sea inspired our best work. Over ouzo or wine, we wove dreams of living permanently in Lesbos. But we each longed for someone with whom we could share bodily the joy that was taking residence in our souls.

In the spring, just about a year after we had separately moved to Lesbos, Jude and I traveled across the island together to Aphrodite's temple. We offered flowers, honey, and wine on the altar we created, pouring out the desire and pain in our hearts, repeating again and again the words Jude spoke first: "If there is anyone in the universe for me, send him to me or me to him."

A few days later I met Nikos, a soulful, intelligent, younger man with an engaging smile and infectious laugh. Nikos loved to talk. He had an intensity that stimulated me to become more aware of what I was feeling in every moment. I called him *polilogas*, "talkative," because that was the quality that most endeared him to me. It was a relief not to have to do all the emotional work in a relationship. Nikos was fluent in French, having lived in Paris for seven years, but he spoke no English. He was patient and helpful with my Greek, and soon the words were slipping off my tongue. Though he was unhappily serving time in the army when I met him, Nikos told me his real love was writing. He was a passionate and persistent lover, and I came to adore his skinny body. After a few weeks, he said he was in love with me. Add to that the rose gold sea at sunset, the heat of summer, the singing of birds, and my own desire: *I felt the Goddess had sent him to me in answer to my prayers.* With him I knew ecstasy in the beautiful island of Lesbos. Watching the stars emerge in the veil of night, Nikos and I imagined an exciting life traveling and writing together after he got out of the army. At the end of the summer, I took my dreams with me to America where I would teach for a semester. When I returned, Nikos would be free.

Everything fell quickly apart when I came back to Greece. I did not understand that when Nikos got out of the army he returned to his addictions. Not wanting to involve me in his life, Nikos tried to end our relationship several times. But I couldn't or wouldn't let go of my memories and my dreams. I kept thinking that somehow the Goddess would find a way to bring us back together. Instead, we drifted apart.

When Nikos left me, the voice of my despair returned. "Look at what a fool you were," it said, *"No one loves you, no one will ever love you, haven't you understood that yet? You might as well die."* The betrayal I felt was not only his betrayal. I felt betrayed by the Goddess who, I believed, had sent him to me *and* by my own deepest intuitions and feelings which had seemed to assure me that Nikos and I had a lasting destiny together. I didn't know how to make sense of what had happened. I thought there must be something terribly wrong with me, something that made me deeply and finally unlovable.

In desperation, I threw myself into an affair with the first man who came along. While it lasted, I was able to hold back the voice. But as soon as he left, it came back. "See," it said, "I was right. *No one understands you, no one will ever love you.*" Several months later, another man appeared.

There were many things wrong in this relationship, but I refused to see them. I needed it to convince me that I could be loved. Our affair went on for close to a year; much of the time I was unhappy. When it ended, all the hurt, anger, and confusion I had experienced when Nikos left came back. I wanted to die.

This time I feared that I really might kill myself. Thoughts of suicide had plagued me throughout my life, surfacing most intensely whenever a love affair started coming to an end. Something had stopped me: my work, my little dog, my friends. Now I was more alone than I had ever been. I had followed Nikos to Athens and had few friends there. My dog died just before I left Lesbos. My work no longer inspired and sustained me. The Goddess I had written about seemed to have abandoned me.

As I struggled with my despair, it seemed like there were two of me: the brave six-foot-tall, blonde, beautiful, successful, strong, competent self with a Ph.D. from Yale and several well-known books on feminist spirituality that most of the world saw, and inside, a desperate creature who wanted only to die. Afraid of that creature's power to annihilate every reason I had for living, I felt that the only way I could survive was to refuse to listen to her, to kill her if necessary, before she killed me. I struggled to push her voice from my mind, falling asleep with the television on, holding on to a lucky stone to protect me, keeping busy so that I would never be alone with my thoughts. It was an uneasy truce. I did not know how or when she might emerge again to destroy me. Underneath, I was terrified. But to the world, I presented (whenever I had her under control) a calm exterior.

I did survive. I adopted a white calico cat and named her Chloe, the Greek word for the green growth of spring. Chloe was painfully small and afraid. Gradually, she gained weight and began to come to me. I started to make new friends. I bought an apartment and threw myself into renovating and furnishing it. I fell in love with two Persian carpets in shades of soft green, pink, and dark blue. I ordered a Louis XV living room set covered in rose and indigo velvet. I sewed lace curtains patterned with doves on a friend's machine. I learned to hammer and nail, to use an electric drill, and to install light fixtures. I painted and refinished furniture, including an antique china cabinet that I found at the flea market. Physical labor was healing, and I created a beautiful home. I planted a garden in the pots on my balcony. Soon it was all abloom. I started having dinner parties, for the first time in my life finding the time to enjoy cooking.

My mother shared my enthusiasm for my apartment, and she and my dad announced that they were finally coming from California to Greece to visit me. Knowing that Mom was coming, I redoubled my efforts to finish my work. Each day, I would say to myself, "Mom will like this. Mom will love that." I understood that my parents' desire to visit me in Greece for the first time in the five years I had lived there was their way of affirming the life I had chosen, a life very different from theirs. I felt that my mother's coming across the ocean to my home would add another and much-longed-for dimension to the healing of our relationship.

During this time, I was vaguely aware of a major problem that I kept pushing aside. I had no idea what I would do when I finished renovating my apartment. I had come to Greece to write more boldly and to love more fully, yet I could do neither. I was afraid to let myself even think about falling in love again, because I feared that I literally would not survive another disappointment. And I could not write. At first I thought my writing block would pass, convincing myself that words were forming inside of me as I tackled yet another project in my house. But the words did not come. I felt that everything I had written in the past was worthless, because, though it had helped others, it had not helped me to overcome the despair that haunted me.

A woman whose name was also Carol and whose life had been changed by my books, wrote me several letters during these years. First she told me about a crisis in her life and its resolution. When she became a travel agent, she said that her dream was to organize Goddess tours that I would lead in Greece. I put these letters in my to-be-answered-file, thinking: someday, maybe, but not now. I remembered my days teaching about the Goddess in Lesbos as exhausting. I had forgotten, or did not want to remember, the ecstasy.

I gradually came to understand that my anger at the Goddess, my anger at life, my anger at love, my anger at myself, had become a bitterness that clogged the well of my creativity. But knowing this did not help. As I went about my days, I felt no desire to write. From time to time, I felt vaguely guilty, as if I ought to be doing more, wondering if I were denying a gift that had been given uniquely to me. But when I thought about the two manuscripts I had written before my last bout with despair, I felt nausea. I was ashamed of the self others viewed as naive. One editor had written that though my memoir of my year in

Lesbos "passed the subway test" (she had missed her stop because she was engrossed in the story), the manuscript as a whole left a "bad taste" in her mouth because she "felt she knew more" (about how the relationship with Nikos would end) "than the writer herself knew." Nor could I bring myself to make corrections on my Goddess thealogy manuscript, given that I felt estranged from Aphrodite.

So I painted the pots on my balcony blue one day and watched television the next, waiting for something to happen, avoiding the question half-formed in my mind—if I was not going to write again, then what was I going to do with the rest of my life?

DEATH

$\mathcal{O}$n the summer day I expected my mother to telephone saying that she and my dad had confirmed their reservations for Greece, she called instead to tell me that the persistent cough she had been complaining about had been diagnosed as cancer. She was going to start treatment, so she and my father would have to postpone their trip. In the next weeks, the prognosis worsened. There was cancer in her lungs, in her uterus, and in her hip bone.[9] My brother Brian called to urge me to come home for Mom's seventy-second birthday in August. He said that though Mom remained optimistic, a doctor friend of the family had told him, "This will be her last birthday, and she won't be here for Christmas." As I hastily packed, I took pictures of every nook and cranny of my new house to show my mother.

When I saw Mom, it was hard to believe that she was dying. Although she had started chemotherapy and radiation treatments, she looked beautiful and healthy. The illness had caused her to lose the extra pounds that had plagued her later years. Her always light hair had greyed to a lovely warm champagne beige. She was cheerful and full of life. She did not look or seem old. In her pink flowered dress with a lowered waistline and full skirt, sitting on a blue velvet chair in the family room, she looked almost like a girl. A sadness in her eyes, evident in photographs taken at the time, was the only indication that she was not well.

When my mother was diagnosed in July with the cancer that took her life in December, she was as happy as she had ever been. My parents' economic struggles during the years of my brothers' and my childhood had enabled them to afford a beautiful home that she loved, and a garden filled with flowers that gave her endless joy. After my younger brother, Kirk, married and left home, my parents fell back in love.

Recent years had brought the birth of three new grandchildren. My father's retirement left my parents free to travel and enjoy life.

When she looked at the pictures of my apartment, Mom seemed distracted, and she didn't say much. I guessed that her energies were engaged in the struggle with her illness, and I understood that she would never share my new home with me. I began to accept the fact that my parents' plan to come to Greece would have to subsitute for their actually coming. Then my brother Brian picked up the photos I had brought with me and commented, "But this looks just like Mom's house." I was pleased to admit that he was right. Though Mom would never visit me in Greece, I would feel her presence in my home.

During my visit, Mom told us she didn't want to die and would fight for her life. She added that she had lived a very happy and blessed life and "if her time was up," she had "no regrets." I was relieved when she said that she did not intend to be attached to tubes, and had signed a living will stating she did not want to be put into the hospital even if she got very sick. Mom confided to Brian that if it became clear that she would not recover, she didn't plan to linger. That was as close as she would come to talking about her death. Mom sent me back to Greece after three weeks, insisting that she felt fine and didn't need any help.[11]

My mother's illness affected me more deeply than I had ever imagined it would. It is one thing to hear from a friend or to read that "the loss of a mother is the hardest loss you will ever face," or that "your mother's death is something you will never get over," or that "the mother-child bond is the strongest bond." It is quite another to learn that what had sounded like clichés when spoken by others are deeply personal truths. Though I loved my mother and enjoyed being with her, it was also true that I had left her when I went to college and never came back to live near her. For twenty-some years I had made my life living apart from her, separated sometimes by the American continent, sometimes by the Atlantic ocean, and never by less than four hundred miles. I was quite unprepared for the depth of feeling her dying would evoke in me.

The knowledge that my mother was dying and that she might never ask for my help tormented me throughout the fall as I tried to go about my daily life in Athens. Whenever I spoke with my mother on the telephone, she insisted that she was "doing fine" and "didn't need help." In the late fall, a friend made me realize that I was not calling or writing my mother as frequently as I wanted to out of fear that I would learn that she was getting worse. I sat down and wrote my mom the truth I had come to recognize: *that I had never loved anyone as much as I loved her and that nothing was more important in my life than being with her in her illness.*

Rereading the letter before sending it, I discovered as I would several other times over the next months, that where I had meant to write "nothing is more important than what is happening to *you* right now," I had instead written "than what is happening to *me*." Shortly after my mother died, I wrote my friend Ellen that "*I died*," when I meant to write that "*my mother died*." Though I corrected my "mistakes," I realized that in another sense they were not mistakes: Mom's dying was a passage I was experiencing with her. Though we were not, in any literal sense, the same person, it was also true that like the Mother and Daughter Goddesses, Demeter and Persephone, we were "in fact, merely the older and younger form of the same person; hence [the] easy confusion."[10]

My mother, who received cards and letters from her friends every day of her illness, said my letter "was the nicest letter" she had "ever received." It enabled her to call and tell me that in fact she wasn't "doing fine" anymore and that she would like me to come "home."

When I arrived the Saturday before Thanksgiving, I was shocked to see that Mom had lost more weight, had very little appetite, took many seconds to get up from a chair, and was losing her hair because of the chemotherapy. Still, I was relieved to see that she got out of bed every morning, dressed herself, came down the stairs, and went out of the house almost every day. She insisted that a friend with a similar cancer had looked worse than she did and was now in remission. Her spirit was so strong that it was difficult not to believe her.

A few days later I heard my mother, standing at the kitchen sink in her light cotton robe, mutter to herself, "I hope I don't have to go through too much more of this." I took the opportunity to say, "Mom, if it gets too hard, I want you to know I am here to help you let go." Her response was abrupt, and her tone was harsh. "I don't want to talk about that," she said. "O.K.," I replied meekly and left the room. A few minutes later she came to me and apologized. "I don't want to talk about it," she insisted, "but I heard what you said, and I appreciate it." The only other acknowledgment Mom made of her dying in those last days was when she said that she and her sister had "discussed 'it' and decided that since neither of us has gone to church in thirty years, we don't expect that God will take much interest in us."[12]

The doctor gave my mother a blood transfusion the day before Thanksgiving. I cooked the turkey for the first time, and Mom made it through the day with flying colors, putting on a silk dress and seeming almost well. On Sunday morning she said she wanted to go Christmas shopping with me. On Monday she and Dad and I went out to lunch with one of her older grandsons and took him to the airport. When we got home, she told my dad she felt tired and went up to bed. She never really felt like getting up again. She slept much of the time and ate very little.

Tuesday night they brought her an oxygen tube. It was not inserted into the nostrils, and it didn't hurt at all. My mother was still able to get up to go to the bathroom and even to come down the stairs to watch television. Dad took her to the hospital on Thursday "to see if they could do anything." Apparently respecting my mother's wishes, the doctor did not consider admitting her. After Mom died, Dad told me that this day was the first time the doctor told him (and possibly the first time the doctor told my mother) that there was no longer any hope. I called my brothers, and they came over for dinner. Mom stayed with us in the family room.

On Friday afternoon, Mom's friend Fran took me out to lunch alone, after Mom said that she wasn't able to come with us. During the summer, I had been invited to join Fran, a round, motherly woman with silver grey hair, my mom, and their eighty-year-old friend Ruth, for a celebration of their August birthdays. We had gone to a fancy French restaurant and ordered whatever we wanted, including two glasses of wine each. When she dropped us back at the house, Fran had tried to give my mother a card "good for one hug." My mother, not a "toucher," had politely refused. As she hugged me, Fran whispered, "You are going to have some hard times. If you ever need anything, you can call me."

Even though I scarcely knew Fran, I had called and asked her to take me to lunch. I needed to cry and talk about my mother's dying. I hadn't been able to talk to anyone about it, because my mother hadn't been able to acknowledge that she was dying and neither had my dad. Fran and I held back nothing as we talked, ate, and drank several glasses of red wine. Fran spoke to me about her husband's dying. "I said goodbye to him after his stroke," she said, "because after that he never was himself again. Still, years later, when he slipped into a coma, he didn't seem to be able to let go. Finally the priest told me I had to go in and tell my husband that it was all right with me for him to die. He passed on soon afterwards."

On the way back from lunch, Fran told me that though we had only gotten to know each other since my mom's illness, she really liked me and felt we had a special openness and ease in communicating. She announced that she was going to "adopt" me. Later I understood my "adoption" to be a symbol and a sign of the mystery I would learn as my mother was dying.

When we got back to the house, Mom sat up in bed and talked with the two of us for some time, even raising her nightgown and joking about her skinny legs. Fran told Mom that it was wrong to think that God would not help her. "God comes to anyone who asks Him," she insisted.

On Friday evening my brother Brian and I moved Mom's bed downstairs because the stairs made her short of breath. That night I worried that we might not hear her if she called, and I slept fitfully. Sometime during the night, I felt her mother, her father, her baby sister who died, and her own baby who died waiting for her.[13] Shortly before dawn I heard Mom call. She was struggling for breath and asked me to turn up the oxygen. Dad came downstairs and turned it up, but it didn't help. As I understood that she was dying, I told Mom that "Gramma and Grandpa and baby Alice and baby Alan are waiting for you." Though she could not speak, she showed me with gestures that she was still conscious. As my mother was dying, I had an absolutely clear sense that she was going "to love." Not necessarily to Goddess or God, not necessarily to Mom and Dad, but simply "to love." I told Mom several times not to be afraid because she was going "to love."

Remembering Fran's words, I turned to my father and said, "Dad, Fran says you have to tell Mom that it's all right with you for her to die." He spoke quietly to her, and a few minutes later she died, peacefully, in her own bed as she had chosen, with my dad and me sitting beside her, holding her hands.

The mystery that I learned through my mother's dying cannot be reduced to a few simple words. Attempting to express what was revealed to me, I turned to a the Hellenistic poem whose rhythms echo from my childhood:

If I speak in the tongues of humans or of angels
but have not love,
I am a noisy gong or a clanging cymbal.
And if I have prophetic powers
and understand all mysteries and all knowledge,
and if I have all faith, so as to move mountains,
but have not love,
I am nothing.
And if I give away all I have,
and if I deliver my body to be burned,
but have not love,
I gain nothing.
Love is patient and kind;
love is not jealous or boastful;
it is not arrogant or rude.
Love does not insist on its own way;
it is not irritable or resentful;
it does not rejoice at wrong,
but rejoices in the right.
Love bears all things,
believes all things,
hopes all things,
endures all things.
Love never ends . . .
So faith, hope and love abide,
these three,
but the greatest of these is love.[14]

When my mother passed from this life she was surrounded by a great matrix of love. As she died, I began to understand that I too am surrounded by love and always have been. This knowledge is a great mystery.[15]

GRIEF

$\mathscr{A}$fter my mother's death, I spent several weeks with my father. A few days before she died, my mother said that she was pleased to hear my father and me laughing and talking downstairs. "I don't want to know what you are saying," she said. "I am just glad to hear that you are getting along." I knew this was her way of saying that she wanted us to comfort each other after she was gone. It was very hard to be together without Mom. And yet, our shared loss drew my dad and me closer than we had ever been. For the first time in my life, I saw my dad cry. I could not help remembering that my mother had explained his outbursts of temper one summer in my early teens by telling me that dad had not been able to cry when his mother died. I will always treasure those days we spent together.

My friends Naomi and Ellen called almost every day to see how I was doing. That was a special gift. And my adopted mother Fran was there to help me sort out my feelings of love and abandonment, to remind me that my mom had loved me very much, and to give me her unqualified love.

A few weeks after Mom died, my friend and colleague of twenty years, Chris Downing, drove up to my parents' house to see me. Over lunch in the grill room of my dad's club, I told Chris the story of Mom's dying. She was visibly moved. "I am working on a book on Demeter and Persephone," she said. "Not now, but in several months, I am going to write you a letter. In it, I will ask you to write the story of your mother's dying in relation to the myth of the Mother and Daughter Goddesses. You will sit down and write the essay in a couple of days." Chris was so calm and definite that I had the sense that her words came from a source outside herself. I remembered our conversation during the next days and months, and it comforted me to think of my story in relation to the stories of the Goddesses.

Just about the time that Greeks have a memorial service, marking the end of the first forty days of intense grieving after a death, my father said I could go home. Back in Athens I felt set apart. I spent a lot of time alone, watching television and working on my apartment. I cried a few tears every day when I thought of Mom, not the hysterical tears of abandonment so familiar to me, but simple tears of sadness and loss. I was aware that though my friends wanted to be helpful, they could not really understand what I was going through. They had not yet lost their mothers, and they honestly admitted that they did not want to begin to think about what that loss would mean. During this time, I asked a friend's mother, whose own mother had died some forty years earlier, if she still missed her. "Every day," was her simple reply.

My next-door neighbor, who lost her mother about the same time, would wear black for a year, following Greek custom. I would have liked to wear black too, as an outward sign that I was going through a difficult time. In fact, I wore black more frequently than any other color that year.

In July, almost exactly a year after I learned that my mom had cancer, Chris' letter came. In it she asked me to expand what I had written about Demeter and Persephone in *Laughter of Aphrodite*. I imagined that she had forgotten what she said after hearing about my mom's dying. I had not. I sat down and in a few days wrote the story of my mother's dying in relation to the myth of Demeter and Persephone.[16] With the writing, my year of grieving, which had begun when I learned that my mother was dying, came to an end.

On the evening of August fourteenth, I went with a friend to a little convent in the mountains in Euvia to celebrate the "falling asleep" of the Panagia, the death and assumption of the Mother of God into heaven. The nuns had taken out a special icon that showed the Panagia lying in her deathbed. As I looked at the icon, the Panagia's image merged with my memory of my mother. I kissed the Panagia, cried, and said goodbye to my mom.

Not long after, I was asked to speak to a group of women and men who were on a "Myth and Mystery" tour of the Mediterranean. I would meet them at Eleusis, site of the Eleusinian mysteries, sacred to the Mother and Daughter Goddesses Demeter and Persephone. I wasn't sure what would be asked of me there, or what I would say. As I left home, I tucked the story of my mother's dying into my blue bag in case

I might want to read it. As it turned out, the tour leaders had been told that they must hire a Greek guide to explain the archaeology of the site. They also said that they didn't think a ritual like the one I had written about in *Laughter of Aphrodite* would be appropriate. So, the only thing left for me to do was to read my story.

I led the group to the sheltered place where there is a crevice in the rock. On this spot, it is said, the Earth opened up while Persephone picked flowers, allowing Hades to abduct her to the underworld. Several years earlier, my friend Judy, the co-director of the institute in Lesbos, had put her mother's ashes into the opening, returning them to the womb of the Mother. I thought of her as I sat on a stone near the crevice. Someone set a bouquet of long-stemmed lavender mums on a rock beside me. The others gathered close around me as I told the story of my mother's dying. My voice cracked several times, and I had to pause to fight back the tears. When I finished, I could see that everyone was with me. Some of them, both women and men, were reliving their mothers' deaths. Others were anticipating what it would be like. Few eyes were dry. The story of my mother's dying had become part of a ritual, shared by others. I was no longer alone. It seemed appropriate that this healing had happened at Eleusis, where so many other stories of mothers and daughters, stories of loss and reunion, death and rebirth, had been told. I picked up the bouquet of flowers and offered a long-stemmed lavender mum to each of the others, saying, "Leave your flower here on the ancient stones, or take it home as a memory of this sacred moment."

Part Two

REBIRTH

The miracle-working Panagia of Paliani with silver hands

If you are squeamish

Don't prod the
beach rubble

· Sappho

〜〜 My trip to Crete in the fall set in motion a series of events that would help me integrate the mystery I learned as my mother died, reconnect me to the Goddess, put me back in touch with the sources of my strength, and restore my ability to hope. What strikes me most about this part of my odyssey is how little I chose it and how much I resisted it. But the Goddess was persistent. She wanted me back.

Discovering the Sacred Myrtle Tree by chance, I sensed the mystery that had enabled it to live for a thousand years. Hearing stories of miraculous cures by the Panagia of Paliani, I allowed myself to hope. In the caves, I began to trust the power of darkness. In the mountains, I felt the Goddess' enduring presence. Taken to the rakí festival, I experienced a sweetness in men that I had forgotten existed.

Deeply moved by my time in Crete, I still was not ready to return there alone. But I had no choice. As I traveled, I found kind words and friendship offered whenever I needed them. Descending four levels into the Skoteinó cave, I discovered a strength in myself I had not known before. The Goddess of the cave was hard as rock. She was darkness. In Her presence what was unknown and unformed was not frightening.

Strengthened by this ordeal, I was ready to face the darkness within, to learn why I often felt hopeless and bitter at the deepest level of my being. A jolt from the past, combined with the skill of my therapists, helped me to see that the roots of my despair were to be found in my childhood.

The psychological insights I gained were also deeply spiritual. The despair I felt as a child had become reflected in my understanding of the cosmos. Though I struggled to be hopeful about life, I deeply believed that abandonment was the human condition.

Understanding my past prepared me to reevaluate my relation to the Goddess. My return to Lesbos was the catalyst that provoked me to recognize *that She had not ever abandoned me. I was almost ready to replace the despair that had shaped my life with the mystery I had glimpsed as my mother died. I began to see how my belief that "no one loves me" had blinded me to reality. Old and new friends were telling me how much I was valued and loved. Still, a piece was missing. I was working very hard in therapy. I was trying very hard to make my life work. I had not yet understood that I could relax and simply live.*

THE SACRED MYRTLE TREE

*I*n October I attended a conference in Crete called "The Future of Partnership." Ancient Crete, the organizers of the gathering believed, had been a peaceful Goddess-oriented culture, where women and men lived in partnership with each other and the Earth. I had been to Crete twice before. While I had enjoyed seeing the archaeological sites and the museums, I was not eager to return to the island. I had not regained enough trust in my work, or in the Goddess, to approach the conference with enthusiasm. I attended only because two friends from my Yale days were coming. Mara, with whom I had politicked to bring the government to investigate Yale for sex discrimination, was one of the organizers of the conference. And Naomi, with whom I had raised lots of hell in the field of religious studies and shared many personal crises for twenty years, had received funding from her university in Canada to participate. Carol, the travel agent, wrote to say that she too would attend. I agreed to meet with Carol reluctantly, because I still felt no desire to lead the Goddess tour that was her dream. Once again I would find myself moved by the powers of the Greek land in ways I had not anticipated.

The magic began shortly after the conference ended, when Naomi and I and three others set out in a rented car to explore the island. We had only been on the road about forty minutes when we saw a sign pointing to the left that said "Paliani Nunnery." Four of the five of us agreed to take the detour, so we set off down a winding dirt road that climbed up the side of a mountain.

The Paliani nunnery is built around an open court with a church in its center. The steps leading to the cells that ring the courtyard were filled with pots of flowers in bloom: sweet-smelling basil, gaudy pink geraniums, and headily aromatic white jasmine. The black-clad nuns all seemed to be much less than five feet tall and over seventy years old. Dark-haired, four-foot-ten little Naomi must have felt right at home. I felt like Alice in Wonderland.

The sound of running water drew us to the Panagia Myrtiá, a very old myrtle tree with shoots sprouting up from the roots and curving together to form a massive, intricately woven trunk. A stone wall enclosed the sacred space around the tree, and a small icon of the Panagia, the All Holy, the Mother of God, in a glass case was attached to its trunk. On the branches of the tree were crutches and body braces, testimony to the healing power of the All Holy Myrtiá. A hand-lettered sign said, "Please pick only the dry branches from the tree. Those who do so will be blessed." I deciphered this for the others, and enchanted, we each picked a small twig.

We were approached by a sweet-faced nun, shorter than Naomi, who appeared to be in her fifties. She told us she was the youngest of the nuns. "Almost all the sisters are very old and most of them are sick," she said. "No one has joined us in many years." "But what will happen to the tree and this place if no one else comes?" I asked. "The Panagia will provide a solution," she replied determinedly. "We pray for it every day," she added. "The tree is holy," she told us, "because the icon of the Panagia was found in it. When they tried to put it in the church, it kept returning at night to the tree. Finally the nuns understood that the Panagia wanted to be worshipped in the tree. "The tree is over one thousand years old. Put a twig from the tree in your car when you leave," she cautioned. "It will protect you on the road."

She unlocked the doors of the church with a large iron key and pointed us toward the icon of the Panagia on the iconostasis in the front of the church, on the left side. It is a life-sized painting on wood of the Mother and Child. Her robe is a deep dark red, and across it are stretched two long chains on which earrings, rings, bracelets, and other votive offerings are suspended. One gift of two ornate silver haloes crowns the heads of mother and baby. There are also four silver hands and two tiny silver feet affixed to the icon. I held up my hand and discovered that it was exactly the same size as her silver hand that rests against her robe just under her breast, where it points, perhaps, to her baby.

We approached the icon in turn. Each of us felt her power—even Mardy who had not wanted to come to the convent, and Naomi, who describes herself as a Jewish atheist. "That icon seems very alive," I said to the nun who remained near the door of the church. "I felt an energy field all around it." "It is powerful," she said. "It has performed many miracles. You can see all the jewelry that has been offered to her." "I've always wondered about that," I said. "Are the gifts given when you make a prayer or after your prayer is answered?" "After," she answered without hesitation. "The purpose of the gift is to declare the icon's power. Just recently, a couple came here to baptize their baby. They brought a big candle. This couple, who live in Athens, had been married for seventeen years without having a baby. They were both doctors. They had tried everything. Then they came here and prayed. A year to the day later, the woman gave birth to a son. That is why they brought the baby here to be baptized. Yes, this icon has performed many miracles." I translated for my friends, each of whom allowed herself to believe that just maybe the icon would work her miracles for us.

We each bought a candle, approached the icon, and made a special prayer. As I stood again before the Panagia with the silver hands, I was moved to ask for something I had given up hope of ever finding. When Naomi turned back toward me, I could see that her eyes were wet. "What did you pray for?" I asked. "I can't tell," was her reply. In the end, none of us told the others what she had asked for. That seemed to be part of the mystery. Leaving the monastery, we remarked on how lucky it had been that we had seen the sign and turned left off the main road.

MYSTERIES

The next day we set out to visit the caves of Eilitheia at Amnissos and Agia Paraskeví at Skoteinó. As we drove along the coast toward Amnissos, I recalled that caves have been understood to be sacred from the dawn of religion. When people knew Earth as their mother, the cave, the opening in the Earth, was her vagina and womb, the passageway to her deepest mysteries, the secrets of birth and rebirth.

The Eilitheia cave is in the hills above the ancient port of Amnissos. We arrived in the morning, accompanied by the guard who came with us to unlock the gate. The cave has one large, long room, with a wide mouth, and a low ceiling. There is a belly stone near the entrance that women rubbed to insure conception. Near the center, in shadowy darkness, are two stalagmites, one squat and the other tall, surrounded by the remains of an ancient wall built to enclose the sacred space. The guard told us they were worshiped as the Mother, seated, and the Daughter, standing. Their heads were chopped off by fanatical Christians.[1] In the back of the cave are pools of water, probably used for healing.

As our eyes adjusted to the darkness, we felt that we too had entered into the womb of the mother. Naomi sat by the Daughter stalagmite, while I leaned against the Mother. We chanted to Her and sang, aware of the bemused but accepting presence of the guard who retreated to the entrance of the cave and waited patiently for us. As we turned to leave, Mara crouched at the cave's entrance to take a picture, her short full body the image of the Mother Goddess, her wispy blonde hair capturing the light, crowning her like a halo. Slowly, we emerged from the cool depths, the place of ancient mysteries, into the light and warmth of the midday sun.

We visited the Skoteinó cave in the late afternoon, after lunch and a refreshing swim in the sea. To reach the cave, we ascended into the mountains, passed through the small village of Skoteinó, and turned right down a dirt road. Above the cave is a small church dedicated to Agia Paraskeví, the patron saint of eyesight. I had been there eleven years earlier on her name day, July 26, so I knew that locals celebrated the saint's festival first in the church where they decorated her icon with basil, and then in the cave, where they roasted a lamb, sang, and danced. It is possible that this cave has had a continuity of worship from Minoan times up to the present day.

The first time I visited the cave of Skoteinó, which means "dark," I thought it was one huge, high-ceilinged, cathedral-like room, adorned with stalagmites and stalactites. I felt the cave's mystery, even though I did not follow the boys who were going into its darkened recesses with flashlights. This time, I wanted to go farther in. Mardy said that she had explored caves in the United States when she was younger and offered to lead the way. Mara spoke to two German men in hiking boots as they came out of the cave. They said that the cave had four levels, but it was a bit tricky to get down all the way.

Once inside, only three of us decided to try the descent. My editor Marie, unsure of her footing in the Eilitheia cave, stayed near the entrance. Naomi, afraid of the unknown, perched on top of a large rock formation at the back of the first room with her candle, watching. Mara, Mardy, and I braced ourselves for an adventure. We did not know what awaited us in the dark. Beyond the first room, there was no path. There was still some light from the entrance, and we had candles and small flashlights. We climbed and slid, finding our way in the darkness. The rocks were cool, damp in some places where water had dripped from the ceiling of the cave, but not really slippery. There were no sharp edges because all the rocks had been smoothed by water. We encouraged each other until we got to a place where we could see that the next descent would be through what looked like a hole or a narrow opening. Up to that point, we still had some light from the entrance of the cave, and the space was wide with high ceilings. The final passageway was unknown, frightening, yet inviting. We paused, our eyes fixed on the dark place, thinking about whether or not to go on. Mardy broke the silence, saying that we ought to turn back because it was getting dark outside.

I made the ascent more rapidly than the others, my body urging me on until I reached Naomi. As I walked slowly up the path that climbed through the first big room, I saw two women before me with candles, and two behind me, coming up from the depths, their candles lighting their way. The image of Persephone coming up from the underworld with her torch flashed in my mind. I felt that the Eleusinian mysteries must have begun here, or in a place very much like this.[2]

RELUCTANT GUESTS AT THE DIONYSIAN RITES

That night Naomi and I left the others in Heraklion to catch their planes while we set off for three more nights and days in Crete. Naomi had suggested that we spend the first night in the guest rooms of Paliani, but when we got there about nine P.M., the convent was closed, the gates locked tight. We couldn't rouse a single nun, though we knocked loudly and called out. In the nearby town we asked someone to telephone the nunnery, but either they didn't have the right number, or none of the nuns was near the phone. We learned that there were no hotels or rooms for rent in the nearby towns. The locals urged us to drive back to Heraklion, but we decided to drive on through the mountains to our next day's destination, Zaros. Kostas, one of the waiters in the restaurant nearest the butchers' shops in the old market in Heraklion, had promised us that we would spend several beautiful days there.

Zaros is in the Psiloritis mountains, not far from the ancient Minoan town of Phaistos, closer still to the Kamares cave, where beautiful black pottery, decorated with red and white flowers and spiral designs, was left with offerings of grain, wine, and oil. We hoped to climb to the Kamares cave on donkeys. Zaros is known in central Crete for its spring water, served everywhere we went. Our hotel had a working water mill, still patronized by old farmers on donkeys bringing grain for grinding. The two restaurants near our hotel served mountain trout and salmon, raised in fresh water ponds.

We had been warned that the Kamares cave is four hours from a nearby town, the trail unmarked. We would have to leave early in the morning with a guide. When we arrived in Zaros, we realized that we were very tired from the conference. We decided to put off the Kamares cave to another time, and to spend our first day by the hotel pool nestled amongst the mountains, and the next, hiking the Zaros gorge.

The Psiloritis mountains are bare rock, whitish and grey above the tree line, wild, but worn by time into rounded shapes. We found our breath taken away, just sitting and looking up at them. The first evening we took a short walk to a nunnery at the edge of the gorge, lit candles again, and on our way back, stopped to ask about dinner at one of the tavernas.

Our dinner of fresh fish, salad, potatoes, local wine, tiny Cretan olives, and paximadia, a hard Cretan bread which must be wet in a bowl of water, was just exotic enough to be interesting, and tastier than we had anticipated. After we finished, the waiter invited us to share another pitcher of wine offered by a man I recognized as the shepherd with whom I had spoken earlier about two lambs that, I rightly guessed, were just a day old. We were joined by the second waiter. We spoke again in Greek, and I translated for Naomi. The two young men said that they were best friends and had just gotten out of the army. The sweet light-haired one, who obviously had a crush on me, was named Themis, while the handsome dark-haired one with the long eyelashes was Nikos.

When they discovered that Naomi and I were writers, the two young men were intrigued. "Our village has a very interesting history and many interesting customs," they said. "If you would like to come back and write about it, we will introduce you to all of the old people." "This must indeed be an interesting village," I said to Naomi as I translated, "because usually when they learn I am a writer, Greek men say 'write about me.' These two seem genuinely interested in having the story of their village written." Few of the young people in Lesbos even recognized the value of the culture they were rushing to replace with American jeans and rock and roll. "The two waiters seem to be very close," Naomi commented after a bit. "They are obviously best friends," I replied. "Men in this culture have closer friendships than you usually see among men in America."

When we finished the wine, Themis and Nikos offered to give us a lift back to our hotel on their motorbikes, suggesting that we could all have coffee in the hotel restaurant. When we got to the hotel, they continued on. "What happened?" I whispered to Themis, the light-haired waiter. "Nothing was open at your hotel, so we're looking for another place," he said. I wondered what Naomi, perched on the back of the motorcycle in front of me, was thinking. We drove through town and turned down a dirt road, arriving at the Zaros water factory. "We wanted to show you this," they explained. Naomi said, "O.K., but then you must take us back." The small factory where fresh water is put in the ubiquitous plastic bottle had only a few workers on the night *shift.* Still, our boys seemed very proud, telling us that they had both worked there before they went into the army.

Leaving the factory, we continued on the road that headed out of town. "Where are we going?" I asked, wondering what we had gotten ourselves into. "Just a minute," Themis said as he got off his bike in front of what looked like a small house in the middle of nowhere. "We need to go back," Naomi said as she got off the other motorcycle. "I said that already," I assured her. "I don't know what is going on." "Come inside," Themis said, gesturing us to follow him. "We want to show you how they make the rakí (the clear ouzo-like drink preferred in Crete). This is the still," he continued, as he showed us into a small dark room lit only by a glowing fire. "After the wine is pressed, they put what is left into barrels like those you see over in the corner. Six weeks later, when it is fermented, they bring it to a still, where it is heated over the fire. The steam that rises is directed through long, curved pipes, and comes out as rakí," he said pointing to the various parts of the mechanism.

"I want to go home now," Naomi said. "First you must come and taste the rakí," the boys said, guiding us through a narrow doorway into a second somewhat larger room. A couple of men got up and offered us their Greek-style wooden chairs with raffia seats. Rakí was passed to us, followed by baked potatoes with lemon and salt, eaten with the fingers, and passed on. "They say they are sorry, but they've eaten all the meat," Nikos said apologetically. Naomi gestured that she wanted to go, but at that moment she was passed half of a juicy red pomegranate. She took a few seeds, ate them, and handed the pomegranate to me. "I guess this means we stay," she said, giving me a meaningful look. I knew she was thinking of Persephone who had to spend part of the year in the underworld because she had eaten the pomegranate seeds given to her by Hades. "Kostas is the best singer in Zaros," Nikos said, gesturing toward a small wiry man with a mustache, who was singing and playing the stringed instrument called a Cretan lyre. A younger boy with curly dark hair and big round eyes played the guitar, but was just learning. "Zaros has the best singers in this whole area," Themis said proudly. "They play in all the nearby villages."

The Cretan songs that we heard, called mandinatas, involved a kind of two-line couplet sung by one man, followed by another sung by another man, and so on around the room. The boys explained that whoever distills rakí must throw a party for his friends and welcome anyone who shows up. Our party included most of the unmarried men in the village, because a young man was making rakí. "But another night, or tonight at another still, it might be old men. It all depends." We were the only women. Naomi and I were impressed by the warmth and affection expressed among the men in the room. Many of them sat unselfconsciously with their arms around each other, as our young men did from time to time. We felt that we were privileged to be included in a men's mystery. "Robert Bly, eat your heart out," Naomi said. "This is the real thing."[3]

The two boys whispered translations of all the songs from Cretan dialect into Greek to me, and I whispered the English translation to Naomi, again remarking on their concern that we understand their customs. While both Naomi and I expected songs about wild Cretan mountain men, violence, and vendettas, we were pleasantly surprised to learn that most of the songs sung that night were about men suffering from unrequited love. "I have worn out many pairs of shoes climbing over the mountains to get a glimpse of her," chanted one man. "My goat's udders are sore because I sit and think of that girl instead of milking my flock," responded another. All the while cups of rakí, baked potatoes, and pomegranates continued to be passed.

"We don't sing like this in America," Naomi commented. "That's too bad," Nikos responded. "We sing out our joy and our pain. What do you do with yours?" What indeed? we wondered. All night long, Naomi and I were entranced by unfamiliar rhythms, unexpected sentiments. "This is not the underworld," one of us said to the other, as we were pulled up to dance. "It is the Dionysian festival." [4]

The next day we hiked the gorge slowly, stopping frequently to recall the mysteries we had experienced the night before and to breathe in the energy of the mountains towering above us on both sides of the dry riverbed. Several groups of hardy Germans passed us. This was not a place for speed. It was a place to savor. A holy place. "Crete has given us so many things in such a short time," we kept repeating to each other.

It was with great reluctance that we left Crete the next day, knowing that we would return. When I met with Carol in Athens, I agreed to lead a Goddess tour to Crete.

CHALLENGE

*I*n the spring it became clear that I would have to travel to Crete to make plans for the Goddess tour. I had hoped that one of my friends would be able to come with me, but in the end I had to go alone. Though I regularly spend a great deal of time by myself, I had a number of fears: I knew I would be doing a lot of driving, and I hoped I wouldn't get too tired; I wondered what it would be like eating all my meals in restaurants without company; and I wanted to go back to the Skoteino cave, but I was afraid it would be too dangerous.

The night before I was to leave for Crete, I found myself slipping into despair. I was trying so hard to accept my life as it was, trying not to want the companion I didn't have and felt I would never have. But having to go to Crete alone made me feel vulnerable. Without warning, I began to hear the voice I had worked so hard to suppress, telling me that *"No one understands you, no one will ever love you, you will always be alone, it is just too difficult, wouldn't it be easier just to die?"*

When my Greek friend Melpo came over to meet me for dinner, she sensed my depression. "The way you feel is not right," she said to me as I picked at the black-eyed peas we had ordered in a local taverna. "If I were going to Crete now, I would be happy. But I have to stay in Athens and work in the bank. I'd love to be as free as you are. I'm going to tell you something you may not want to hear. Sometimes I feel the way you do, but I have decided to help myself. I think you should join my therapy group. I think you need to help yourself too." I thought about our recent conversations about Melpo's women's therapy group. I always found something that helped me in the stories she told. Still, I was skeptical. "I have tried therapy," I began, "and it didn't help. I understand what my problems are, but it doesn't do me any good. I feel that life has passed me by. It's too late. I'll always be alone" I said, knowing that I sounded tense, bitter, and close to tears. "Don't you think I've been many years in therapy?" Melpo countered angrily, her green eyes flashing. "Don't you think I know that many therapists are stupid? But in this group I am changing. You know that. Last year I didn't even like to be around women. The group has helped me to understand that my father taught me to hate women. I am a woman, too. He taught me to hate myself. I think this group can help you." I looked at the tall, determined, sometimes intimidating woman sitting across from me, and thought back to the many times she had cancelled our plans to get together. I knew that she probably wouldn't even be having dinner with me if she hadn't started liking women better. I tried another tack. "But don't you speak Greek in the group? I don't think my Greek is good enough." Melpo responded bluntly, "If you want to help yourself, your Greek is fine. If you don't, it will never be good enough."

TRUSTING THE DARK

$\mathcal{T}$o my surprise, when I arrived in Crete I enjoyed getting into the car every day and going exactly where I wanted to go, at my own pace. I did get tired driving, so I rested for two days in the seaside village of Mochlos. Naomi, who longed to come back to Greece, asked me to write a journal about my trip for her, and between that and planning the next day's itinerary, I had plenty to do at meals. I felt like Naomi was with me as I wrote to her of my adventures.

A few days into my trip, I decided to go back to Skoteinó. On the way to the cave, I thought about those who had come there before me. For early humans, caves provided shelter from wind, rain, and heat. In the Neolithic era, the time when human presence is first documented on Crete, people lived and buried their dead in caves. Though archaeological evidence is lacking, it is hard to imagine that they did not enact rituals in the caves' shadowy depths. When people moved out of the caves, they continued to bring the dead there, no doubt feeling that they were returning them to the womb of the mother. Later still, people brought votive offerings to the caves: in the beginning, small ceramic bowls and pitchers for the offering of fruits of the earth and the pouring of libations. Called "simple gifts to the deity of fertility" by archaeologists, they also express a complex sense of the connection between the womb of woman and the womb of Earth; the understanding that all life comes forth from the darkness; and perhaps also the hope that what is dead—seeds, human bones, the human heart—can be transformed, reborn, in the darkness.[5]

When I arrived at the Skoteinó cave, it was the middle of the afternoon. There was no one else in sight. I imagined that if I fell or broke a bone, it would be days before anyone found me. I was afraid, but I also knew that it wasn't really dangerous to get down to the third level where I had gone with the Mara and Mardy in October. I made a prayer for protection in the little church of Agia Paraskeví and decided I would go as far as I felt safe. I would descend with a candle and extra matches, leaving my flashlight behind, because the candle illuminated the nearby space while the flashlight was better for looking into the distance. I quickly made my way down the path to the spot on the rock where Naomi had watched our earlier descent. From there I slowly climbed and slid down over the rocks in semi-darkness. My fear and anticipation melded together into a solemn determination. No sisterly giggles this time.

After a while I found myself at the bottom of the second level, looking down a steep rockface to the third level, a large round room with stalactite formations emerging from the shadows on the wall high above me, capturing the last light from the mouth of the cave. From where I sat, I could see the dark hole that appeared to be the opening to the fourth level. I felt that it would be dangerous to go any farther, so I decided to stay where I was, sitting on the rocks looking down. I was very pleased to have gotten as far as I had on my own.

I asked the Goddess of the Skoteinó cave what I was meant to do with the rest of my life. My writing block showed no signs of ending. If I wasn't going to write, what was I going to do? I asked my question again and again. I also prayed for the healing of the fibroids that had been discovered in my uterus. As I was bleeding, I offered a drop of my menstrual blood to the rocks. I felt the power of the cave and my own power in conquering my fear. But I didn't hear an answer to my question. I asked again. Still no answer.

The third level beckoned to me, and I decided to ask if it was safe to go farther. I immediately received an answer: "*Stay close to the rocks, and you will find your way.*" I understood this to mean that if I stayed close to the walls of the cave, where I could lean against the rocks for support if necessary, I would find a safe path. I got down to the third level easily and went to the dark place, the opening to the fourth level. I started to slide down. The passage way was about the length and width of a double staircase, in some places less than my height. I was in total darkness. Then there was another turn, and my candle lit up a large white stalagmite formation: the aniconic image of the Goddess. It was in the center of an oval room, perhaps twenty feet wide, with high ceilings.

The stalagmite formation was taller than I was and perhaps six feet across. I sat on the floor, leaning against Her, and extinguished my candle. It was completely dark. I had reached the center. The womb of the Goddess. I repeated my prayers. I don't know which was more powerful: this place, or conquering my fear in order to get there. I supposed it had always been the combination of the two.

In the silence, I heard sounds at the entrance of the cave. I thought that others had come, so I began my ascent. Later I realized that the sounds were the cooing of several pairs of doves[6] that live near the mouth of the cave. As I emerged from the depths, I knew that this was a journey I had to make alone. I might not have received the answer to my question, but I felt an inner strength I had not known before.

FLOWERS OF SPRING

$\mathcal{T}$oward the end of the trip, I returned to Zaros, stopping at the Palianí nunnery on my way. I had since read that the nunnery had been known as ancient (palia) in 668 C.E. when mention was first made of it in extant records. When I arrived, the convent was teeming with new life. Bees buzzed around the flowers which spilled out of pots on the steps leading up to the cells. The Sacred Myrtle Tree had many new green shoots and leaves and was coming into bloom, hundreds of tiny white blossoms with cascading stamens.

I looked for the sweet nun with whom we had spoken in October and learned that her name was Evgenia, the Gracious One. She greeted me warmly and introduced me to the abbess, who gave me a small cross carved from the myrtle tree. To me, it looked like a woman with upraised arms. I was also given a photograph of the icon from the church. The nuns insisted that I stay for lunch.

I expected a communal meal at the long refectory table in the dining hall, so I was surprised to be served alone in the kitchen behind it. "All the nuns eat in their own cells," I was told. "They have their own kitchens." My lunch was fresh artichoke hearts and potatoes stewed in tomatoes and olive oil, thick slices of bread, and feta cheese. I learned that the nuns once farmed the convent's land themselves, but now that they are all older, they rent the land to others in exchange for fruits and vegetables, olives, oil, and cheese. After finishing my meal, I reluctantly left for Zaros.

If I had wondered whether the mountains of Zaros would be as powerful as they had been on my first visit, a late afternoon walk down a farm road was evidence enough. The power of the mountains was palpable. The next day I hiked the gorge again. It was even more beautiful in the spring. Camomile, thyme, sage, oregano, and other fragrant herbs and flowers grew along the trail, filling the air with a scent that reminded me ever so faintly of maple syrup. Apparently alone, I began to sing, "The hills are alive with the sound of music." "We all come from the Goddess / And to Her we shall return." "She changes everything She touches / And everything She touches changes." Gurgling water appeared in the gorge about halfway up the trail. As before, I stopped frequently to gaze up at the white and grey rock of the mountain on both sides of the gorge. I gave thanks for being alone with the mountain.

On my way back from Zaros, I stopped again at the nunnery. This time I was greeted as an old friend by gentle, intelligent Evgenia and her robust cellmate with the contagious laugh, Kaliniki, which means Good Victory. I sat with them in the kitchen of their three-room "cell," reception room, kitchen, and a small room with three narrow beds. Kaliniki was cleaning artichokes. Evgenia offered me chocolates and sweet bread. We laughed that all of the doorways, and even the porch roof of the second story of the convent, were far less than my height. "I could never live here," we joked. While I knew that in other ways too, I would never be able to live there, I wondered if the Panagia would call me to help these nuns in the future, or in some other way make me part of her plan to help the Sacred Myrtle Tree survive.

GIFTS

*W*hen I returned to Athens a few days later and unpacked the treasures from my trip, I took out a copy of the larger of the two Minoan Snake Goddesses found at Knossos, which I had purchased in Heraklion. About thirteen inches high, she wears a long skirt and an embroidered apron. A tight bodice accentuates her full bare breasts. A large snake crawls up one of her outstretched arms, down her back, around her buttocks, up over her shoulders, and down her other arm. A second snake slithers around her breasts, encircles her belly, and comes to rest on her tall headdress. Her eyes stare calmly ahead and her palms are open, sending her power outward. I set her on top of the buffet in my living room, beside the Snake Goddess that I already had. She too wears a tight bodice, full skirt, and embroidered apron. Her eyes stare straight ahead as if she is in trance, and she holds two small writhing snakes in her hands.

The Snake Goddesses from Crete call to mind a time when women were not afraid, when our power to bring life forth from the darkness was recognized as sacred. I stepped back to get a better view of the two Goddesses guarding the center of my home. It felt right. Then I seemed to hear a sigh of relief: the two Goddesses thanking me for putting them together. It was as if they were saying: "We belong together, we were together for the rituals at Knossos, we lay together under the earth for millenia, we do not like to be apart."

I continued to unpack, and placed a blue bowl with sculptured birds in the center of the buffet, beneath the Goddesses. I placed twigs from the Panagia Myrtiá, stones and pottery shards picked up along the way, and herbs and flowers from the mountains of Crete, in the bowl and set it on a circle of lace made by one of the nuns of Palianí. A framed photograph of my mother laughing and a second, of her mother, were already on one side of the buffet along with three pairs of my mother's ceramic birds. I went out to buy a silver frame for my photograph of the Paliani Panagia, and put her on the other side of the buffet. Later I would add a photograph of my adopted mother, Fran.

I remembered that the Snake Goddesses were found with shells, suggesting their connection to the sea. I went to my collection of shells and found four similar small striated ones and arranged them around the bird bowl. The composition lacked balance, so I added two larger rose-colored shells from my Aphrodite rituals, choosing them reluctantly, because they were the only remaining pair.

It took me a few days to realize that I had unconsciously created an altar. I added three pink candles and two dark blue votive lights. I dedicated the altar to the Cretan Goddess, calling Her Vritomartis, one of the non-Greek names found in the Linear B tablets from post-Minoan Crete, and Skoteiní, the Dark One, after the cave of Skoteinó, Panagia Myrtiá, and Panagia Palianí. I lit the candles on my altar, renewing my connection to the source of life and death.

A few days later, I sensed that I received answer to the question I had asked in the Skoteinó cave. In a letter to a friend, I wrote, "I see myself spending more and more time in Crete, exploring the sacred mountains and sacred caves, returning to visit the sacred tree, learning about Minoan archaeology and Cretan folklore, possibly one day buying a house in Crete and spending part of each year there." As I reread the words I had written, I understood that the Goddess of the Skoteinó cave had answered my question. When She said: "*Stay close to the rocks, and you will find your way,*" She also meant: "*Stay close to the the mountains and caves of Crete, and you will find the path of your life.*"

PROMISE

$\mathscr{A}$s I settled back into my life in Athens, I realized that I had been transformed in ways I could not fully name. Traveling alone in Crete—descending into the darkness of the cave—had given me the courage to face whatever was dark and unknown inside me. I was ready to try once again to stalk my despair in the therapy group Melpo had recommended.

Charis Kataki, one of the two leaders of Melpo's group, invited me to come in for an initial private appointment. Her office was in a house on a residential block in an upper-middle-class neighborhood of the Athens suburbs. I was a bit early for the appointment and waited nervously. When Charis opened the door of her sunny, plant-filled office, I took in her external appearance: attractive rather than beautiful, elegantly dressed, short, light-haired, several years older than myself. As we seated ourselves in her office, Charis told me that she had studied in America and invited me to speak English if I would feel more comfortable. I said I would rather speak Greek so she could get a sense of whether I could keep up with the group.

Since Melpo had told me that Charis was married and had children, I assumed she would find little to empathize with in my story, but I plunged ahead. I told her I felt bitter about my life. I found it too difficult to live alone. I said that if I had known when I was younger that I couldn't have love, family, and a career, I would have chosen love and family. I felt the feminist movement had betrayed me because it told me that I could "have it all." I had ended up with nothing. As a Goddess feminist, I couldn't get the kind of academic job that would have been satisfying. My writing, which had once been a lifeline, seemed meaningless. It was too late to have children. I didn't have a husband, and now I was probably too old to meet anyone. I told Charis about the voice that told me "*No one understands me, no one will ever love me, I might as well die.*" I said it felt like that voice came from a separate personality over which I had no control. I was afraid that one day I might give in to the voice and commit suicide. Charis asked me about my parents, my education, my marriage, my decision to live in Greece.

"You made the right choice when you moved to Greece," Charis commented when I finished. "Greeks live from here," she said, touching her belly. "You needed to learn that." Then she looked me in the eyes and said simply, "*No one should have to live with the kind of despair you feel.*" I was stunned. No one had ever told me that before. Charis said that she knew I had tried everything I could think of to change my life—from therapy, to changing the world, to changing my country, to changing God. She said that she and the group would help me face the source of my despair and get beyond it. That didn't seem possible to me. I assumed that the sadness and despair I had always felt were deeply rooted in my personality, impossible to change. Still, I was intrigued. Could it be that someday I would feel differently?

SURPRISE

$\mathcal{A}$bout that time, while walking with a friend in Plaka, the oldest part of Athens, I heard my name called out and turned to see Nikos, the man whose leaving had catalyzed my depression. It was like seeing a ghost. He had a bit of grey in his short black hair, and he looked a little older. But he was as skinny as ever, his golden-brown eyes still had a twinkle, and he was nervous and intense. Nikos pulled me away from my friend and said quietly in the soft basso tones I well remembered, "I was in a community for a year and a half. I have been out for a year. I don't take drugs anymore." "That's great if it is true," I said, remembering his lies. "It's true," he said. "After I got out of the community, I came by your old apartment, but you had moved. Why don't we exchange phone numbers, so that we can meet and talk." I gave him my number and folded his into my wallet. Remembering the many times I had called him in the past, I thought, I won't call you.

The next day he called me. I was still in shock. So much was stirred up inside of me—memories, hopes, dreams, anger, self-criticism, recrimination, guilt, combined with the sheer joy of seeing him again. My feelings were confused. When Nikos suggested that we get together, my anger spilled out. "I won't call you," I said. "I have called you enough times for a lifetime." As I hung up the phone, I wondered if he would apologize.

REVELATION

I was afraid about what might happen if I saw Nikos. Would I fall in love with him again? Would I want to commit suicide if he left me again? As I started to talk about my feelings in therapy group, Charis, whose therapeutic style is aggressive, cut me off. *"The feelings you had when Nikos left you were too extreme. They were not about him."* She paused, "Didn't you say your father was an alcoholic?"

I was stunned. "I said that my grandfather was an alcoholic," I stammered. "My father's personality may have been shaped by his father's alcoholism: because his father was out of control so much, my father felt he always had to be in control."[7] "Talk to us about your father," Charis interjected. "My father and I are very different," I began. "He is a traditional patriarchal father figure, I am a feminist. He is right-wing. I am left-wing. I think he loves me, but I don't know if he is proud of what I have accomplished." "I don't think you are so different," Charis interjected. "I know we are alike in a lot of ways," I responded. "We're both very intelligent. We both work very hard. We're both very demanding of ourselves and others." I paused. "I thought we had grown closer after my mother's death. The two of us were with her when she died. Afterwards I stayed with him, and we talked openly for the first time in years. We shared our grief and our love for Mom. He told me he couldn't talk like that to my brothers. Last year I went home for the anniversary of Mom's death. We had a good cry together. My dad almost never cries. After that, it seemed that we were getting along really well. But just before I left, my father told me that although he loved me and planned to give me my mother's beautiful antique gold watch, he also wanted me to know the ways in which my behavior over the past several weeks had irritated him. My first offense was that I kept moving a chair in the kitchen—and one night he tripped over it. I was stunned. I thought I was putting the chair where it belonged; he never told me otherwise. This was an example for him of my 'aggressive manner' which I also displayed when, while I was cooking dinner for him and friends of the family, I said, 'Dad will set the table,' instead of asking nicely if he would. I thought we were working together on dinner; I thought that what I said was friendly, not aggressive. I had been trying so hard to get along with my dad, and I thought I had finally succeeded. But I hadn't. I collapsed in tears. He went out. I cried all night long. I started to feel that he and my mother had never really loved me. That incident was typical of my relationship with him." I continued: "His behavior was always unpredictable. Just when I thought I was getting closest to him, he would explode. Just when I thought I was doing the right thing, he would criticize me. I never seem to be able to please him."

We talked about my relationship with my father for a while. The other therapist, Patrick, the gentle Frenchman who had helped me to feel comfortable in the group, because he, like me, speaks Greek with an accent and some mistakes, intervened. "I think I see the dynamics of your 'family myth,'" Patrick began. "Because his father was an alcoholic, your father felt that there was a 'badness' passed down through the male side of the family line. For some reason, he felt this 'badness' could especially harm the girls in the family. This was a 'family myth.' It wasn't true," Patrick said, looking at me intensely from behind his thick glasses. "But your father believed it was. So whenever he felt close to you, he had to create a distance. He did this to protect you from (what he felt was) his 'badness.' Your perceptions were not wrong. It was precisely when your dad felt closest to you that he withdrew, got angry, or criticized. This must have been very confusing for you as a little child. The truth is that your father loved you very much. But he was afraid to express it, because he felt he would hurt you. In fact, he hurt you while he was trying to protect you. If you can understand this, maybe it won't hurt so much from now on," he concluded, smiling tentatively and nodding, as if to ask me if I understood.

What Patrick said sounded strange at first, but when I thought about it over the next few weeks, it began to make sense. I was amazed that although he scarcely knew me, Patrick had so quickly intuited so much. I had not ever mentioned that my father's brother was an alcoholic—yet this was further "proof" that the "badness" was passed down to the males in the family. Nor that when I was a child my dad's sister had had a nervous breakdown and became addicted to tranquilizers prescribed by her doctor. Once her husband had told me that her problems stemmed from her relationship with her father—the father's "badness" had indeed harmed the female child in the family. I began to see that my father was the only one of his siblings who had managed to lead a relatively "normal" life. The other two had gone "out of control." No wonder my dad struggled so hard to stay in control of everything and everyone. He had done so at great cost to himself and others, but he had survived. Both of his siblings were dead. I began to admire his strength.

Patrick's depiction of the family myth and its dynamics provided insight into why my brother Kirk had been drawn to Mormonism, a religion that prohibits alcohol and stresses self-control on the part of males. It also helped to explain why I had had so much difficulty with men. Many of the men I had fallen in love with had serious psychological problems. In a mixed-up way, I was drawn to them, feeling that if I could heal their pain, perhaps I could also heal my father's, and then I could get the full expression of the love that he had never been able to give to me. In addition, my father's pattern of withdrawing love just when we were closest had made it very difficult for me to make a realistic assessment of relationships. Because love and rejection were so intertwined in my relationship with him, I had a hard time knowing the difference. My mother had always told me that my father loved me, even though he often didn't show it. No wonder I had so readily accepted erratic and unloving behavior on the part of the men I loved.

Gradually over the summer, this new knowledge, combined with other smaller insights gained in the group, began to take root in my body and in my feelings. I began to understand that although I was loved in my family, I had also been greatly damaged by my father's behavior. Before it had always been one or the other: either I was loved or I was unworthy of love. Now I began to see that my parents loved me, but because they were limited, they often could not express their love in clear and open ways.

Slowly the feeling that I was somehow deeply and finally unworthy of love began to diminish. As this happened, the dynamics of all my relationships started to change. When I stopped looking for constant verification that I was worthy of love, I began to see others more clearly. It was as if I had gone through life with a veil over my eyes, and that veil had been lifted. For the first time in my life, I was able to separate myself from others. I was able to see that, just as I as a little child had not caused my father's reactions to me, neither was I, for the most part, the cause of other people's behavior. I began to see that when others disappointed me, more often than not, it was because of their limitations, not mine. This new understanding was incredibly freeing.

There were times when I still fell back into my old patterns, nights when I still wondered, "*Will anyone ever really understand me or love me?*" But those times were fewer. The balance had shifted.

WORDS WITH YOU,
APHRODITE

In the middle of the summer, work called me back to Mythimna, to Lesbos, to the place where I had felt claimed as a priestess of Aphrodite, the place where I trusted and served Her, the place where I had begun the love affair whose ending plunged me into the despair that closed the wellspring of my creativity and stopped my writing.

I had been asked to give two lectures to a group of graduate students studying archetypal psychology in Greece and would meet them in Lesbos. I was uneasy about returning to Mythemna after an absence of four years. I felt abandoned by friends from the village who had not written or called in recent years. I was still very angry at Aphrodite, and yet I had agreed to speak about Her to the group in Lesbos. I was angry at myself for letting myself be so disappointed in love. It would hurt to return to the place where I had lost so much.

Three nights before I was to leave for Lesbos, while looking at a framed print of the Panagia Myrtiá, the All Holy Myrtle Tree, I started wondering if myrtle trees really could grow to be over one thousand years old. I decided to look up the myrtle tree in a book.[8] To my great surprise and distress, I read that the myrtle tree was sacred to Aphrodite. Given how angry I was at Aphrodite, I felt this was a dirty trick. "My" tree was "Hers." I didn't want Her to have anything to do with my altar, with my renewed relationship to the Goddess, with the sacred twigs from my sacred tree. I was furious. I began to feel heavy and depressed. I left my air-conditioned study and went to the living room where I lit the candles on my altar, hoping this would change my mood. The temperature was over 100 degrees, so I returned to my study. There I picked up another book, *Gods in Our Midst* by my friend Christine Downing,[9] and restlessly flipped through the pages where she writes about Hermes as a trickster. I felt more and more agitated.

I returned to the living room, pulled up a chair before my altar, and began having words with Aphrodite. "I hate you," I said. "Se misó," I repeated over and over again in Greek and English. Then I continued, "You abandoned me. You left me to die. Not once, but many times. You left me in the underworld. All I did was love you, worship you, introduce others to you through my writing and my rituals. And look what you did to me." I wanted to scream at the top of my lungs, but I thought of the open windows and the neighbors. Instead, I lay on the floor and moaned. In the silence that followed, I heard Her say: "*I did not abandon you. Who do you think led you to the Palianí nunnery? You were so angry with me that I had to disguise myself for you to find me. But you did find me there. Do you remember your prayer? You asked for what you believed I had taken from you. You knew I was there. I did not abandon you. The path you are on now is not easy, but I will be with you all the way.*" As I lay on the floor, I felt She was also telling me that one day the prayer I made at Palianí would be answered too. I wondered if that was true or whether it was just my own desires speaking. . . .

Then I had a vision of the fibroids in my womb dissolving and flowing out with my period. I saw these fibroids as dead babies, the baby I had wanted to have in my forties, my baby brother who died, and finally, baby Carol who had been so disappointed so many years ago that she gave up hope and wanted to die.

EVERYONE IS WAITING
FOR YOU TO COME BACK

*B*ack on Lesbos, I felt the island's beauty seducing me as the taxi traveled up into the winding mountain roads lined by pine forests, and down again through the olive groves toward the Gulf of Kalloni. As we drove along the flat marshy lands at the edge of the sea, I asked the taxi driver to turn down the unmarked dirt road leading to Aphrodite's temple. We passed a few small farms and soon crossed the place where the spring pours water onto the road. The temple was locked, so I scaled the fence, and quickly wedged a silver ring, two snakes entwined, between the ancient stones, my acknowledgment of the gift Aphrodite had given me a few nights earlier.

As we resumed our journey, passing through the outskirts of the town of Kalloni, and then climbing back into the mountains, I thought about Axiothea, Ellie, Nena, and Photeiní, my Greek women friends, who had been like family during my Lesbos years. I had called and written, trying to maintain the connection. At some point I stopped, after I realized they were not calling me or sending cards. I felt rejected. When I thought of the other townspeople, I felt shame. Everyone knows my love affair failed, I said to myself. Now they will look at me and say, "She is old, fat, and ugly. She'll never get what she wants." I felt sick when I imagined walking through the town alone. The taxi descended again into olive groves and soon the bare rock of Petra, with a tiny white church to the Panagia at its crest, emerged against the sea. In a few short minutes Mythimna's hill came into view, the fortress crowning its summit. Soon the taxi deposited me at the Delphini Hotel outside town.

Karin, one of the two women who greeted me when I arrived, suggested a swim. Though it was already late afternoon, the grey-blue sea beckoned. Floating in the embrace of the salty water, I shared my fears with Karin, who was teaching one of the classes in the summer program and also had recently become the lover of the program's director, Jennifer. Her blonde hair glistening in the sunlight, her eyes filled with pain, Karin told me about the problems she and Jennifer had been having with the students and faculty in the group. "They may be responding to my feminism or to our lesbianism. There is a great deal of anger." "It could also be their response to being in a foreign culture," I countered. "We always had problems with the groups we brought to Lesbos." Our conversation continued to be open and intimate as we swam farther and farther out. Karin told me the story of how she and Jennifer met. I shared the story of my descent into the Skoteinó cave in Crete. "I sense your life changing as we speak," Karin said, affirming my journey. I was relieved when she suggested that we go shopping together before meeting Jennifer and several of the other faculty members for dinner.

As we entered town, we ran into a man about my age, a former restaurant owner, once stunningly handsome, who had had affairs with many foreign women. He was walking with his four-year-old daughter, and, I noted, he was developing a paunch and beginning to bald. If I am aging, so are they, I mused. He greeted me with genuine warmth, introduced his daughter, and asked why I had been away from Mythimna for so long. As Karin and I walked through the narrow streets of the marketplace, this scene was repeated. Shop owners ran from their shops to greet me. Everyone said, "Where have you been? Why have you forgotten us?" And, "You look more beautiful than ever."

Axiothea, Ellie, Nena, and Photeini were delighted to see me and wanted to be with me whenever I had any free time. They each claimed to have lost my phone number and address. I wasn't sure whether that was true or not. Jennifer later suggested another explanation: people from small towns have difficulty maintaining friendships with those who come into their lives and go, because it is painful for them to know that you have left and they never will. The reasons became insignificant. I had not been rejected. I was much loved. I could feel it.

The black-clad widow Maritsa put the gift I was receiving into words when she hugged me outside the tiny booth from which she sells cigarettes, candy, and postcards. "*Karolina,*" she said, "*you never did any harm to anyone here. Everyone loves you. Everyone is waiting for you to come back.*" I thought of her words that night as I stared out over the dark sea, waiting for Axiothea and Giorgos to meet me for a late dinner. She was right. The only person who had judged and rejected me was me. I began to cry tears of relief and joy. That night I cried myself to sleep.

When I got back to Athens, I developed a cold. After a few days I realized that clear water was dripping from my nose. I was releasing tears.

FORGIVENESS

*W*hen Nikos received the card I sent him from Lesbos, which said simply, "Greetings from a place I remember and you remember—I would like to get together some day," he called immediately. "I thought you didn't want to see me," he began. "I thought you thought that," I said. "That's why I sent the card." During this call which lasted for more than an hour and ranged over many subjects, Nikos apologized. "I don't see my old friends," he began. "When I left the community, there were only a few people I wanted to see, because I valued them. You were one of those. That's why I came by your house. I wanted to tell you that I know you gave me only love, care, and help, and I gave you very little in return. *You didn't fail. I failed. I am sorry.*" I was stunned. I can't remember exactly how the conversation continued. But I do remember that somewhere in what followed, I said, "I needed to hear that." "Thank you." "I accept." And, "My therapist says that the sense of despair I felt after we broke up was about something that happened long before I met you." Overcome with emotion, I ended the conversation. We agreed to meet. When I put down the phone, I realized that my nose had stopped running.

Family obligations intervened, and we had to cancel our first meeting. I was disappointed, but in the end I was glad of the extra days. While I was waiting to see Nikos, something drew me to read Downing's chapter on Hermes again. This time the following words leapt out at me, "He[rmes] is *there*, at all transitions, marking them as sacred, as eventful, as epiphany. Our awareness of Hermes' presence opens us to the sacredness of such moments, of those in-between times that are strangely frightening and that we so often try to hurry past."[10]

Seeing Nikos, speaking with him and hearing his apology, had shaken me deeply. I was beginning to see that I had woven a tale with threads of self-judgment, guilt, and rejection, similar to the one I had woven about my Mythimna friends, that simply was not true. I had not failed. He had. The only failure I could justly attribute to myself was not seeing that Nikos had lied to me about taking drugs. And I could forgive myself for that. I had never been around drugs. I didn't know the physical signs of drug use. I didn't know how drug addicts lie. If only I had been able to say four years ago when Nikos left me for drugs, "I didn't fail, he did," I would have been fine. I could have gone on with my life.

The fact that I didn't had nothing to do with him, and everything to do with me. I began to sense that I had been severely traumatized when I was a child. Whatever had happened, I had felt a betrayal of trust so deep that I had not wanted to go on living. The feeling of rejection that stemmed from that trauma was easily triggered in me in intimate relationships with family, friends, and, especially lovers. I did not know, and might not ever know, what had actually happened back then when little Carol felt she died or wanted to die.

But now I held the thread that could unweave the cloak of pain and disappointment that had cast such a deep shadow over my life. Every time I began to feel rejection, I would ask myself: am I being rejected now? Or have feelings that have nothing to do with what is happening now been triggered in me? I would fight the temptation to lose myself in ancient pain.

ON THE FAR SIDE
OF DEATH

When Nikos and I did meet for that first time, we talked intensely for three hours, seated across from one another in my living room on a hot summer morning. No small talk. Every word measured. Every word heard and examined. There was a moment when I felt rejected, followed by another when he did, but we got past them. After Nikos left in the early afternoon, I cried for the rest of the day and into the evening. At some point I called Melpo. "I guess I am sad," I said. "You don't sound sad," she said. "Maybe you are releasing something. Let yourself cry. Don't try to analyze it." I cried myself to sleep. In the next days I wrote a poem.

Today I have been crying

All day I have been crying
hours and hours I have been crying
and still it is not done.

Today I have been crying
because you said: I am sorry
because you said: You gave me only love.

Now I see:
my love was clear and pure like crystal.
My love was shining.

You say: Cry. It is good to cry.
You say you are touched by my words.

You say you would rather be my friend
in honesty and truth
than my lover only for today.

I ask you to hold me
as a friend
your arms embrace me
as a friend
you don't let go
words form in my heart
you say: put your belly next to mine,
that is where the pain is.
And that is where the pain is.
You hold me as a friend
and it is not sexual

something breaks up
inside me
I feel your arms
your belly
your self-control
your strength
I open.

I cry to see you strong.
I cry to see you clean.
I cry to see you clear.

I feel
release
as you hold me

on this threshhold.

I drink water
tears roll down my face
pain frozen inside
melting.

We talk of love and sex
and you say:

If one is disappointed in love
life goes on.
I say: I have felt my life
coming to an end.

You say: life goes on.
I do not say
but know you know:
it was not like that for me
when you took drugs and left.

I cry and cry.
I say: I looked for your obituary.
Dead of an overdose
syringe beside the body.
And here you are
across this room
alive.

I can't stop crying
for love
that tempered by so much pain and betrayal
endures
and delights
to see you smile.

The tears do not stop.
Now I know it was my obituary
I expected to find.
But I am alive.
And this is love
between friends.
Not death.

THANKSGIVING

*I*n the next days, I went to the new altar on my buffet and added a double frame with two photographs: one was a picture of me in a white dress, taken in Mythimna when I was radiantly happy and in love, the other was of the rose gold sea at sunset in Lesbos. I called the Snake Goddesses by the names I had discovered for them, Vritomartis and Skoteiní, and spoke the names of the Panagia Myrtiá, Panagia Palianí, and Aphrodite. I smiled at my mother and at her mother and at my adopted mother and at myself. I lit the candles on the altar.

> *I thank the Goddesses*
> *for life*
> *and for love*
> *for love that does not die*
> *for love that does not ever abandon us*
> *for life that has been lost*
> *and given back.*

I have come full circle. I feel so much love for so many people and from so many people. The wellsprings of my creativity are opening again. I begin to know what it means to trust life.

Part Three

PILGRIMAGE

Women dancing in a meadow with lilies, Goddess descending from
the sky, snakes, an eye, a chrysalis, and a shoot in the background

And their feet move

Rhythmically, as tender
feet of Cretan girls
danced once around an
altar of love, crushing
a circle in the soft
smooth flowering grass

· Sappho

Though I had been to each of the sacred places we visited on the pilgrimage I led to Crete, it was different to share them with other women. The many faces of the Goddess were reflected not only in images in the museums, but also in the icons of the Panagia, in the eyes of the Cretan women we met, and in the tears and laughter, courage and fear, anger and love of the women on the tour. Each day brought a new revelation of the Goddess: vital as the myrtle tree, dark as the cave, enduring as the mountains, in chains yet continuing to give, deeply cherished throughout time. She was the air we breathed, the ground we walked upon, the water we drank, the food we ate, the highest mountain, the deepest crevice, the surrounding sea. As we drew strength from each other and from Her, our rituals grounded us in the Earth, restoring an ancient female power that should have been our birthright.

In retrospect, it is easy to see that the loss of control, exhaustion, and illness that I suffered throughout the pilgrimage are the classic elements that mark the beginning of initiation. Historians of religion explain that the outwardly strong individual will not give up control and become open to revelation unless pushed to the brink. The rite of passage can be an ordeal that tests physical and psychological strength. Exhaustion and illness may also be an opening to transformation.

It is not coincidental that my initiatory illness occurred during a pilgrimage I made with other women. I had to become tired and sick, to have control taken from me, in order to learn that I am not alone and do not have to do everything for myself. The lesson of my pilgrimage was affirmed each day by the women I traveled with, confirmed by each person who offered love and support along the way, and symbolized in the rituals at Gournia and Zakros.

Nor was it by chance that I was required to accept help from men. The Goddess of ancient Crete did not exclude men, but encouraged women and men to live together in harmony and peace. Though our quest was necessarily made as a group of women, we were reminded that in the end (whether we are homosexual or heterosexual), we must also learn to live with our brothers.

Throughout our journey, I tried to let go and accept the love and help that was continually being given to me. Still I was tired. Still I was sick. Finally, overcome by exhaustion at Kato Zakros, I was led in the serpentine path of an ancient dance, then joined by others in a ritual. This was the moment of my initiation in Crete.

PREPARATION

In the fall, I prepared myself to lead the pilgrimage in search of the Goddesses of Crete I had been planning for a full year. I looked forward to introducing the thirteen women who would join us not only to the history and archaeology of Crete, but also to the healing power I had experienced there. I did not realize that for me, too, the trip would be a spiritual journey.

In traveling to Crete we hoped to gain a vision of a culture where women walked bare-breasted, proud of their bodies, without fear of violence. When I told Soula, an attractive woman who owns a jewelry shop in Sitiea in eastern Crete, that we were a group of women searching for the ancient Cretan Goddess, she understood immediately. Raising her arms as if holding writhing snakes, and then lowering them and cupping her breasts, she said, "Do you mean the Goddess with the snakes? She was the first feminist." "Exactly," I replied. Soula understood intuitively that in seeking the Goddess, we were searching for a power that would take root in our bodies, a deeply female power, both spiritual and sexual.

The culture of ancient Crete was very different from our own. As classics scholar Lucy Goodison has written, in ancient Crete "we find a society which was in many ways unusual: where women predominated in religious and perhaps social life, where some settlements seem to have been communal, and where there is surprisingly little evidence of military weapons and fortifications."[1] According to Goodison, patterns of dominance were introduced into Crete by Mycenean warriors from the mainland, whose presence began to be felt after 1600 B.C.E., the time when the warrior-kings first established themselves in fortresses in the Peloponnese. Even though the Cretans built large complexes called "palaces" during the years 2000–1450 B.C.E., the society we call "Minoan" nowhere celebrated warriors or warfare. There is no evidence that they had a king. Indeed, current theory proposes that the so-called palaces were communal centers where rituals of the agricultural cycle were celebrated, and where planting, harvesting, and distributing of food were organized.[2]

The ancient Cretans venerated the Goddess as the source of life, movement, and beauty, and as Jacquetta Hawkes writes, a sense of "the grace of life" is expressed in the lively, rhythmical forms of Minoan art.[3] While the Goddess is more prominent than the God, and women play central roles in the cult, men are never depicted as subordinate. Both women and men are portrayed as proud, graceful, beautiful, strong, and frankly sexual. Apparently both men and women took delight in their bodies and came together without the specters of fear and self-loathing, dominance and contempt, that have marred the relations of the sexes throughout recorded history.

Lacking a model for genuine equality between the sexes, some have imagined that ancient Crete must have been a matriarchy where women ruled over men and perhaps even sacrificed them. But there is no evidence that women subjugated men in Minoan Crete. Habits of dominance and subordination seem to be a product of militaristic societies,[4] and the military was never depicted in ancient Cretan art.

Why is it so hard for us to imagine a society without dominance? Is it because we long for it with all our hearts? Is it because the very idea that such a society could have existed calls into question patterns of behavior we have thought to be unchangeable? Is it because we cannot bear to think that we do not live in the most progressive and evolved societies that have ever existed on this planet? Is it because we are afraid to face the pain that living with violence and the fear of violence has etched into our bodies and souls?

The vision of a world where women were not afraid would open old wounds in all of us. And yet, some or all of the women would be expecting to have a good time, to experience the joy of new vision, but not the pain that gives it birth. The expectations of those who left home and came halfway around the world "in search of Her" would be high indeed. I would be leading rituals whose goal was nothing less than the appearance of the Goddess! I was afraid the women on the tour would be disappointed if She did not appear to them in full living technicolor.

I knew that those who were open would learn important lessons "from the rocks" of Crete. But I also knew the teachings would come when they were least expected, would not always be welcomed, and might not be recognized until after the trip was over. Not everything would be easy. It seemed important that we stay grounded, find and feel the earth, the bedrock, and the water, under our feet, in our travels and in our rituals.

Living in Greece had made me keenly aware that North Americans approach life with a desire to control. In contrast, Greeks shrug their shoulders, throw up their hands and say: "ti na kano;" "what can I do?" Greeks understand that we do not control the conditions of our daily lives, let alone our destiny or fate. Certainly not the Goddess. I hoped that rather than rushing to import our American-based practices to Greece, we would be patient, wait, and listen. I knew that if we expected nothing, much would be given.

Carol Lee Sanchez, a very wise part-Pueblo Indian woman, once said to me as we both stood outside a ritual circle of mostly white Goddess women: "You white women know how to raise energy, but you don't know how to ground it. We Indian women ground energy naturally *because we are part of the land.* I get tired trying to ground for all of you." I stood outside this circle because I got a headache while participating in it. I knew then that I would never again want to raise energy that I could not ground.

My most important task as leader would be to help the others stay grounded. I would suggest that we begin our rituals with simple libations of milk and honey, water and wine, gestures that acknowledge our connection to Earth as Giver of All. In this way we would connect ourselves to the traditions of Crete and Greece and open ourselves to the revelations that would come forth from the Earth.

EVERYTHING
UNDER CONTROL

$\mathcal{A}$s I prepared to leave for Crete, I was forced—dragged kicking and screaming is more like it—to relearn the lesson about control I had hoped to share with the group. Although I was extremely upset and angry as control was taken out of my hands, I now see that the experience of losing control was a necessary part of the path that I would travel on *my* pilgrimage.

The night before the trip was to begin for me, I went to my therapy group. I felt very good because everything seemed to be falling into place. I had spent the week fine-tuning the details of the trip: I would finish packing my clothes in the morning, leave the house just before 1:00 P.M., hail a cab, stop at a Greek govenment office to pick up a permit for free admission to the archaeological sites, meet our Athens travel agent Rena to pick up the groups' return tickets for the ferryboat ride, find another cab, and arrive at the airport in time to catch my plane at 3:30. I had a list of ten or so phone calls I would make from Heraklion in the late afternoon or the next morning; in the evening I would go to the house of some Cretan friends for dinner; the next day I would visit the museum and Knossos again to refresh my memory; in the late afternoon, I would be ready to meet the women.

I shared with the therapy group that I was feeling very good about my life. I said I was thankful for the lessons I had learned over the summer, grateful for the help they had given me. When I finished, Charis, rarely as sympathetic as Patrick, looked skeptical. She asked the group to respond to my statement. One of the other women said she felt there was something false in what I had said: I seemed to be trying too hard.

For reasons I did not understand at the time, I started to cry uncontrollably. The group came to me and held me, but I did not feel comforted. When I got home, the voice I was still struggling to hold back came forth. *"No one understands you, no one loves you,"* it insisted. I knew this was not true, but I could not stop crying. This time I was not crying tears of release, but tears of despair that came from a well of ancient pain. I tried to tell myself that I had no reason to cry, but I couldn't stop. I sobbed myself to sleep and began again when I woke up. I was certain I would forget something as I finished packing, and I was afraid that I would still be crying when I met the group the next day.

I closed my bags just in time to rush out and hail a taxi to take me downtown. Rena, a tall dark-haired Greek American with a no-nonsense manner, was waiting in front of the government office with her motorbike. She embraced me warmly before I ran up to get the permit to speak at the archaeological sites. My mission accomplished, Rena handed me the tickets and some other information. Always warm and enthusiastic, she told me that she knew the trip would be a great success and reminded me to call her if there were any problems. She left me standing on the corner with my bags, assuring me that I would have plenty of time to find a taxi to take me to the airport.

But I didn't find a cab. A pre-election bomb had gone off at the Athens bus depot the night before, and people were afraid to take the bus. All the taxis that passed me had passengers, and none was going to the airport. After forty-five minutes, my arm still stretched out in front of me, I started crying again as I realized that I would probably miss my flight to Heraklion.

I called Rena, who checked with the airport and informed me that due to the upcoming elections when all the Greeks go back to their villages to vote, there were no reservations available to Crete for the next ten days. My sobs became hysterical. I knew that even if I could get a first-class cabin on the ferryboat, I would not be able to sleep, because I am claustrophobic in small, airless spaces. Rena came to collect me with her motorcycle, loaded it with three of my bags, and instructed me to walk several blocks with the remaining one to a street where we could find a taxi to Pireaus, the port of Athens. She assured me that I would at least be able to find a third-class ticket on the boat. I didn't want to go on the ferry, but Rena insisted, hailed a taxi, and virtually pushed me in.

I was just barely holding back the tears. The tall, good-looking taxi driver spoke kindly to me until I told him about missing my plane. He called the airport to see if the plane was late, then kept up a conversation all the way to Pireaus, where he stopped the cab and went in to the ferryboat office with me to be sure I got a first-class ticket. Later it seemed that he had been sent by the Goddess to help me.

I managed to control my tears as I climbed up the narrow staircase of the boat. When I went to my cabin to drop off my bags, I discovered that it was larger than I had expected. If I were alone in the room, I might be able to sleep. I checked later and saw no sign that others had been assigned to the bunk beds across from the single bed I had claimed with my bags. But after dinner, I found two other women in the cabin. I slammed the door in frustration and collapsed in the narrow hallway in hysterical and angry tears. I felt totally unable to control my crying. Without sleep, I might not be able to regain the self-control I would need to begin guiding other women to the archaeological sites and holy places of Crete. I slept fitfully on a couch in the first-class lounge, waking every hour or so throughout the night.

HELP ABOUNDING

*W*hen I emerged, bleary-eyed, from the ferry boat at about 6:30 in the morning, I was totally surprised to see my Cretan friends, Maria and her husband Giorgos, waiting for me with their car. Maria and I had become fast friends when Naomi and her daughter Natalie and I stayed in their rooms-to-rent in Mochlos over the summer. Now they were back in Heraklion for the winter. I had asked Rena to cancel the date I had with them the previous evening, and I hadn't expected to see them until after the trip. I had never been happier to be met anywhere. As the song says, "You can't always get what you want, but . . . you just might get what you need."

Giorgos loaded my bags into the trunk of the car, and Maria said that we were going home for a big breakfast. Maria sat me down at the kitchen table in their modest apartment, while she moved gracefully around her kitchen, chatting, making coffee, and setting out bread, butter, and jam. "Did you notice that I've lost another ten pounds?" she asked, her hand on her hip, her black eyes flashing. "I'm jealous," I teased. Though Maria and I are the same age, she has a body type—broad shoulders, full breasts, slim hips, not too much of a waist—that has probably always looked matronly. Her husband Giorgos, a tall, somewhat austere former village policeman many years Maria's senior, asked with genuine warmth about Naomi and Natalie. Soon we were joined by their tall, awkward, but good-looking son, Haris, whom Natalie had insisted had a crush on me for a few days during the summer. He too seemed genuinely happy to see me.

After breakfast, Maria took charge as we walked into town to do the things that I had to do: find a pair of walking shoes (I had forgotten to pack the ones I had bought especially for the trip), pick up one extra copy of the guidebook we were to give to participants, stop by the travel agency that was providing the bus for the trip, check in at the hotel, arrange dinner for the group at a local restaurant, buy candles for the caves and incense for the rituals, and stock up on supplies for my period that had started the day before. I don't know how I would have managed without Maria. Luckily, she likes to shop, and we had a good time together—stopping midway through the morning for loukoumades, honey-drenched Greek donut holes.

Maria had put a leg of fresh goat on the stove before we left, and it was ready when we got back. "You can stay with us any time," Giorgos said as we finished lunch. "You are one of ours now." I knew this was an important statement in a culture that makes a strong distinction between "family" and "strangers," the word used for everyone outside the family.

I was deeply exhausted when I lay down on my hotel room bed in the early afternoon, but I had stopped crying. I had not done everything I had planned to do, but with help from my friends, I had done the everything I needed to do.

The group arrived in the late afternoon. When we introduced ourselves before dinner, I was pleased to discover that most of the women were about my age, somewhere in their forties, with a few older and a few younger. They all seemed eager and excited to begin our journey together. I took them to dinner at the ouzerie Maria and I had decided upon in the morning. The waiters brought us plates of cold octopus vinagrette, mussels in tomato and cheese sauce, keftedakia, little meat balls, fava bean dip, tzatziki, cucumber and yogurt dip, taramasalata, fish roe dip, boiled greens, salad with feta cheese and tiny olives, black-eyed peas, fried potatoes, and golden retsina, all served family style. It was quite an introduction to Greek food. Tired from their travels, most of the women went to bed early, but a couple of us lingered over the wine.

LANGUAGE
OF THE GODDESS

$\mathscr{B}$ecause I had not been able to go back to the museum and Knossos on Saturday, I did not have everything "under control" when the tour began the next day. The museum was being painted, and the chronological and thematic titles, such as "Neolithic and Pre-Palace Finds" were not in their expected places on the walls of some of the rooms. Even though I knew the artifacts in the museum quite well, I was forced to open the guidebook to refresh my memory.[5] I felt that I should have known more. Later, several of the women in the group told me that my not knowing every date and detail helped them to understand that the really important things they would learn on the trip were not those that could be memorized or found in a book.

The Heraklion museum was our introduction to the culture of ancient Crete. The others gathered around as I pointed out the small Neolithic Goddesses in the first room. According to many archaeologists, women were the probable inventors of agriculture, pottery, and weaving in the Neolithic period, which in Crete dated from about 6000 B.C.E. to about 3000 B.C.E. As keepers of the mysteries involved in these vital economic processes, women must have held important religious and social positions in Neolithic societies. Women were probably the creators of many of the objects on display in the first room of the museum.

One of my favorites was a tiny ceramic jug in the shape of a Goddess with narrow snakelike arms, who was herself holding a water jug. I reminded the group that the archaeologist Marija Gimbutas believed that the spirals, chevrons, triangles, and other patterns that decorate Neolithic pottery are part of an intricate "language of the Goddess," symbolizing the female body, water, and fecundity.[6] The Earth was the body of the Goddess, and the combination of human, animal, and elemental forms expressed the fullness of Her power.

I pointed out the offerings left at the mountain peak shrines, among them small terra cotta images of female and male worshippers, the women bare-breasted with long skirts and the men wearing a codpiece that accentuated their sexuality. To me these images show men and women as equals—with no implication of one sex gazing on the body of the other as object. In the same case there was a model of three black birds resting on three columns. "Columns like these probably stood at the peak shrines. The appearance of the birds would have been understood as the epiphany of the Goddess," I explained.

In the next room, which had artifacts from the early palace period (c.2000–1700 B.C.E.), we looked at the exquisite large red, black, and white painted pitchers, jugs, and bowls in "Kamares" style. Used for ritual offering of grain, wine, and oil, some of them had been found in the Kamares cave. The group began to understand the language of the Goddess. The spiral designs were snakes, wombs, caves, the mystery of transformation. The sunflowers were flowers, the sun, and the powers of growth.

In the next room was the Phaistos Disk, found in the treasury of the first palace at Phaistos. On both sides of it, are mysterious, untranslated hieroglyphics. Because they are written in a spiral pattern, scholars believe the words may be a prayer or ritual chant. We gazed in amazement at the disk, and at the examples of the untranslated Linear A tablet, that, if deciphered, might provide written "evidence" for what we could already feel in our bodies: that women were not subordinate in Minoan culture.

We were delighted to find the well-known Snake Goddesses in the fourth room, with other finds from the last palace period (1700–1450 B.C.E.). Bare-breasted and holding writhing snakes, they reminded us that there was a time before we were split into virgin and whore and taught to cover our bodies in shame. Seeing them, we could feel ourselves becoming healed from the damage done to our self-images by the stories of Eve and the Snake. Though they are often pictured separately in books, the Snake Goddesses were found together in the treasury where the most sacred objects were stored at Knossos. I imagined that they were placed together on an altar during special festivals, perhaps surrounded by

painted sea shells as they are in the museum. I envisioned lines of wor-
shipers passing by and leaving offerings, perhaps kissing the altar, in
much the same way that contemporary Greeks venerate the icons. The
Minoan priestesses, who enacted the role of the Goddess in rituals, also
dressed in tight bodices, long skirts, and embroidered aprons. Amazingly,
the tight bodice, long skirt, and embroidered apron are still part of the
traditional woman's costume in Crete, though the breasts are now covered by a blouse.

Near the Snake Goddesses, in another case, are two small glazed
plaques, depicting a cow nursing her calf and a goat nursing her kid.
Both the cow and the goat have long horns. "Look carefully at the
horns," I said gleefully. "The archaeologists almost always identify the
horned bovid as the sacred bull, but unless the sex is clearly indicated,
it could just as likely be the sacred cow. For example, the so-called
bull's head rhyton, a libation vessel carved from black stone with inlaid
eyes of rock crystal and golden horns that is one of the most widely
reproduced images of Minoan culture, could just as well be a cow's
head rhyton, an image of the Mother Goddess. Perhaps it was milk or
honey, not the blood of sacrifice, that was poured from its nostrils."

When we arrived in the room where larger-than-life-size double axes
found at Nirou Hani are displayed, we stared in awe. I confided that the
symbol of the double axe remained a mystery to me. Some scholars see it
as a stylized butterfly, others as a double pubic triangle, and still others
associate it with the control of the weather. It is certain that double axes
were not used for animal sacrifice. Large double axes often stood near
altars, and smaller ones were left as votive offerings. The double axe is
sometimes held upright by women or Goddesses, but never by Gods or
men. Perhaps it was used like a lightening rod to draw energy. While I
was speaking, small red-headed Jana and her much taller friend Karen
spontaneously stood between the three large double axes, their arms
raised, bent at the elbow, palms open. With or without written records,
they understood that Minoan culture celebrated female power. Just being
in the presence of its art was changing how they felt about themselves.

RITUALS AT KNOSSOS

*M*y feeling that I should have known more was intensified when we visited the archaeological site of Knossos in the late afternoon. The "palace" of Knossos, which is situated near the modern city of Heraklion, is a labryinthine complex of buildings built and rebuilt between 2000 and 1375 B.C.E. It was discovered and elaborately reconstructed at the turn of the century by the British archaeologist Sir Arthur Evans, who developed many of the theories about the religion and culture of ancient Crete.

I had received permission to speak at the archaeological sites only a few days earlier and consequently had not familiarized myself with the details of the buildings at Knossos. There was no way that I could pretend to "know everything" as I would have liked. To my surprise, the group didn't seem to mind opening their guidebooks and reading together about what we were seing. As I relaxed, I realized that I had many things to add. This was an important lesson.

Sir Arthur Evans, an aristocratic gentleman, believed that he had discovered a king's palace, and he named the culture he discovered "Minoan" after the legendary King Minos mentioned in the *Iliad* of Homer. Contemporary archaeologists challenge his assumptions. Nanno Marinatos argues that the "palaces" were not royal residences, but cult centers used for storage of offerings from the harvest and for celebration of rituals connected to the agricultural cycle. The complex of buildings was a social, economic, and religious center, combining the functions of a farmers' grange co-operative and a community church. Religion and agriculture were not viewed as separate spheres: the Goddess was the provider of agriculture. With elaborate rituals, dances, and processions, the ancient Cretans expressed their desire to live in harmony with the

Earth and its cycles. Seedtime called for propitiatory rituals to ensure the growth of the crops, while harvest was a time to give thanks that the Earth and the Goddess continued to provide.

Marinatos rejects the designation of the complex as a palace, because she found no evidence that there was a king. In the ancient Near East, kings were military leaders. Yet in Minoan Crete there is no glorification of the military, no depiction of the armed king. A fresco of a long-haired youth wearing a peacock feather crown described as a "priest-king" by Evans has been reproduced so frequently that it has become emblematic of Minoan culture. But it has recently been disputed as inaccurately reconstructed. The so-called throne room of King Minos did not exist until the very end of the Minoan period, and possibly was a result of Mycenean influence. King Minos himself lived during the time of the Trojan war, several centuries after the end of the culture Evans called "Minoan." Furthermore, according to Marinatos, the throne room is more likely a part of a shrine complex designed for the epiphany, or highly ritualized appearance, of the priestess enacting the role of the Goddess. The mythical animals called griffins that flank the throne are the companion animals of the Goddess, not the king.

We began our tour of Knossos in the west court, a paved area outside the building complex. Two raised pathways were used for processions, such as those of women and men carrying the fruits of the agricultural harvest, depicted in one of the frescoes we had seen in the museum earlier in the day. At the edge of the court are three large deep stone-lined pits, identified by Marinatos as granaries. Here, a portion of the agricultural harvest was stored in the early palace period, perhaps to be distributed in times of need, or to be consumed in community festivals. The location of the granaries outside the building complex suggests that control of distribution was shared by the townspeople. In the later periods, grain storage moved inside the walls of the temple center, possibly due to consolidation of control by a religious elite.

We approached the temple complex by way of another processional walkway. Monumental steps led up to the columned entry hall. The seven-foot tall limestone "Horns of Consecration" dominate the large open central court. Several of the women felt an irresistible urge—as I had the first time I visited Knossos—to stand inside the horns with upraised arms as the Minoan priestesses must have done. The horns frame the highest mountain in the area, Juctas, where there was a peak shrine.[7] Like all symbols, the Horns of Consecration must have had many meanings. They are the horns of the sacred cow or sacred goat, the giver of nurturance, depicted on the plaques we had seen in the morning. They call to mind the upraised arms of the Goddess or her priestess and suggest the mountain peaks rising above the valleys. They also are the horns of the sacred bull or ram that mated with the females, was wrestled by bull-leapers, and in the late or post-Minoan period, was sacrificed in rituals.[8]

From the Horns of Consecration, we looked down over large open central court, approximately fifty by twenty-five meters, set on a north-northeast axis, where processions and ritual dances must have taken place. On all sides, the sacred buildings were encircled by still productive farm land on the surrounding hillsides. Looking around the court, our eyes paused to take in large pithos jars, four and five feet tall, once filled with grain, wine, olives, and olive oil. The distinctive Minoan columns, wider at the top, painted blood red and black, provided a rhythmical counterpart to goldish grey stones used to construct the buildings.

When we peered into the darkened throne room on the northwest side of the central court, we could almost see the bare-breasted priestess dressed like the Snake Goddesses in a long flounced skirt and embroidered apron, entering the through the doorways of the adjacent room.

We ascended a narrow staircase to the second story, where we were entranced by copies of many of the frescoes we had seen at the museum in the morning. We focused our attention on one that showed women in blue and yellow gowns dancing around sacred trees in the center of a courtyard. Could this scene have taken place in the open court where we had been standing a short time earlier?

After we looked at the reconstructed sacred buildings that surrounded the court, Sue, a raven-haired beauty with clear white skin, who had confided that coming to Crete was a long-standing dream for her, said that she wanted to find the "theatral area" at the northwest corner of the site. I didn't know exactly where it was, but she persisted, and together with the group, she found it: a wide space in the ancient road just outside the "palace," flanked by broad steps on two sides. Sue suggested that those taking part in the ritual processions approaching the cult center must have stopped there to dance, make offerings, or pour libations while others watched from their places on the steps.

As we stood imagining what might have been, several of the women in the group left the place where we had gathered on the steps. Raising their arms, palms forward, with red-haired Jana leading, they began to recreate processions on the road to the theatral area. The ritual had begun, in a quiet way, without anyone planning it.

Later, several of us gathered around a large rock. Robin climbed up and reclined, spreading out her gauze skirt and arranging her long reddish-brown hair. We joined in as she led us in song, spontaneously pouring libations of water, first on the rock, and then on each other, a welcome relief on a very hot afternoon. A sweet-looking woman whom I took to be German, stood near us, watching and smiling. I invited her to join us. As she approached shyly, I realized that she was about four or five months pregnant, just beginning to show. Her "appearance" in our midst seemed to be a blessing.

I was the first to arrive back at the bus at the appointed time, and I fidgeted that the others were late. The bus was hot, so I slipped across the street to look in a tourist shop. There I stumbled upon a terra-cotta copy of the small seated crowned Neolithic Goddess found near Ierapetra that we had seen in the museum a few hours earlier. The original is made of clay that has been burnished to look like stone. According to Gimbutas, her thick snakelike arms and legs and the lines that mark her body identify her as a Snake Goddess.[9] On impulse, I bought her. I did not know that she would be the only image of the Goddess to grace our altars. In the end, I was the last one on the bus.

THE TREE OF LIFE

*T*he next day we visited the convent of Paliani and the Panagia Myrtiá, the Sacred Myrtle Tree. The adoration given to the All Holy Myrtle is a living testimony to the survival of ancient worship of the Tree of Life. Besides the fresco at Knossos that showed costumed women dancing around sacred trees, we had seen a gold ring in the Heraklion museum that depicted women tending sacred trees encircled by stone walls. Long before the Genesis story was written, women celebrated the Tree of Life. Indeed the biblical story was probably written as a polemic against cultures that viewed the Woman, the Snake, and the Tree as holy. Through the nuns of Paliani who plant flowers for the Panagia around the Sacred Myrtle Tree, we are given a glimpse of ancient priestesses who created a garden for the Goddess around the Tree of Life.

As I told the group the story of how the icon wanted to be worshiped in the tree, I shared my feeling that the power of the Goddess could still be found in the images and icons of the Panagia and the female saints. When Christianity prohibited Her worship, the Goddess went to the places where She could still be honored and revered. The images and names are different, but the devotions, prayers, and the offerings have changed little in thousands of years. For me it has been healing to sense the living presence of the Goddess in the icons. The Panagia can become a bridge linking us not only to the ancient past, but to the faith of generations of women who have shared their hopes and dreams, tears and sorrows, with the Mother.

It is no secret that the Panagia, the image of female power, is the most popular figure in Greek piety. Indeed the name "Panagia," does not mean "Virgin Mary," but simply, "All Holy" in the feminine gender.

It could have been, and probably was, one of the names of the Goddess. The name "Panagia Myrtiá" means "All Holy Myrtle Tree" in the feminine gender, and could also be a pre-Christian name.

The Orthodox believe that the "power" of the saint is "really" present "in" the icon, as the Roman Catholics believe that the body and blood of Christ are "really" present "in" the bread and wine of communion. I explained that Greeks cross themselves and kiss the icons when praying. I encouraged the women in the group, to do so as well, recalling that the cross is an ancient symbol of wholeness.

As I looked around the nunnery, I was struck by its similarity to the so-called palace at Knossos. Both had an open court enclosed by sacred buildings. Both were surrounded by productive fields. Like the ancient Cretans, the farmers who lived near Palianí came together to celebrate their connection to the Source of Life in festivals that coincide with harvest times. On the days celebrating the Assumption of the Virgin (August 15) and the Birth of the Virgin (September 8), festivals are held at Palianí. It is possible that the open court at Knossos could have had a sacred tree. Perhaps the "religious elite" that Marianatos imagined living at Knossos were, like the nuns of Palianí, a group of people who dedicated themselves to creating and preserving a sacred space at the heart of their communities.

Because I did not want to do anything that might offend the nuns, I had planned a simple ritual. I brought multicolored ribbons from Athens and suggested that each woman tie a ribbon to the tree, perhaps adding a small votive offering, and make a wish. I wound the ribbons around a piece of cardboard so they would not get wrinkled. When I passed the ribbons around the bus, I suggested that each woman take the ribbon that was on the top of the card, rather than choosing the color she preferred. I had hoped to get a deep dusky rose ribbon that for me symbolized Aphrodite and the joys of sexuality, but instead I got a sky blue one.

When we got to the sacred tree, I decided to share the story of my experiences with the Panagia Myrtiá. I sat in the shade of the branches of the tree, just outside the stone wall that enclosed the sacred space. I felt vulnerable telling about my disappointment in love, of my loss of faith in myself, in the muse that inspires my writing, in the Goddess, in life itself. I spoke of the healing power I had sensed in the Sacred Tree and in the icon of the Panagia in the church. And of my anger on learning that the myrtle tree was sacred to Aphrodite, the Goddess I felt had betrayed me so mercilessly. I told how I had screamed out my anger and heard Her say that She had never abandoned me. I wasn't sure how the others would respond to my story, but later, a number of the women told me that my willingness to speak so honestly had enabled them to open to their own pain and offer it to the tree.

I suggested that we each meditate on why we had received the particular color ribbon we got, before tying it to the tree. As I looked at my light blue ribbon, I remembered that I had purchased a bright blue bead, protection against the evil eye, the day before. In many cultures, blue is the color that wards off evil. In rural Greece, a blue eye is always pinned to the clothing of a baby when it is taken outside the house. I found the bead in my bag, threaded the blue ribbon through it, and tied it to the tree, asking the Goddess for protection. I now understand that I had received the color of protection because I was in the process of shedding an old skin, an armor of control. I would become soft and vulnerable like a newborn. The blue ribbon was a promise that I would be safe.

After we had tied our ribbons to the tree—others too having added votive gifts—and offered our prayers, we formed a circle around the ribbon-bedecked tree. Someone spoke about the color of her ribbon. Soon we each shared the gift we had discovered in the color we had received. Then we held hands and Robin asked if she could sing. An aged nun stood outside the circle watching us and smiling sweetly. I realized that our feelings and our gestures were very familiar to her, and it did not matter that we sang to the "Goddess," rather than to the "Panagia" because she would not understand our words. After singing several songs Robin taught us, we grounded ourselves against the tree. I realized that one of the women was sobbing and went to comfort her. Several other women clung to the tree for some time.

It was with great reluctance that we left the convent. The next day, Marian and several others told me that if the trip had included only Paliani, it would have been enough. It was not only the beauty of the tree that was so moving. Deep inside us, myths that associated Woman, the Snake, and the Tree with evil were being shattered.

TASTE THE SWEETNESS

$\mathcal{A}$fter we left the convent, our bus climbed into the Psiloritis mountains, where the Kamares and Idean caves are found. Our destination was Zaros. My body tensed with anticipation as I thought about hiking the gorge, the rakí festival, the haunting sounds of the Cretan lyre. I felt calmed by the sound of rushing water during our lunch at a taverna next to the mill.

Though I was tired, I could not rest after lunch. The mountains called. Even though I knew the way and she didn't, I allowed Patricia, who seemed at home on the path, to take the lead. I was delighted to see the confidence and determination in her gait as her long legs took control of the trail. Letting her go first gave me a chance to relax and absorb the healing strength of the grey and white mountains rising steeply on both sides of the gorge.

The next morning we traveled down through the mountains to Phaistos. The "palace" is situated on top of a hill in the middle of a richly cultivated valley surrounded by high mountains—a graphic demonstration of its role as an agricultural center. The ancient stones were bathed in the clear light typical of Octobers in Greece. The Kamares cave, a site of pilgrimage in Minoan times, was visible as a black smudge high up on the cloud-covered peaks of Mount Ida. It was there that the first examples of delicate black and red painted pottery known as Kamares-ware had first been found.

As we entered the archaeological site at Phaistos, which was not reconstructed as at Knossos, we began to recognize familiar details: the raised processional paths cutting across the open courts outside the building complex, a theatral area with stepped seats or stands, large circular granaries near the entrance, huge ceramic pithoi, storage jars, still in place inside, the large central court situated on a north-northeast axis. The many rooms and buildings that had seemed like a maze at Knossos became more comprehensible as we saw patterns repeated. Images from the museum came to life as we imagined women in flounced skirts and men in loincloths walking slowly on the processional paths carrying offerings of grain, wine, and olive oil in large red, white, and black Kamares-ware jars decorated with spirals and sunflowers.

We were forced to open the guidebook again to locate the shrine rooms on the west side of the court. The group didn't seem to mind being asked to read archaeological details from the *Blue Guide Crete*; in fact some of them commented that it was fun to discover the sites together. I began to relax a bit more. I was doing just fine, even though I didn't "know everything."

We proceeded through the workshops to the exquisite group of connected rooms with paved floors of alabaster tiles lined with red plaster. These rooms, which would have been decorated with frescoes, were on different levels, approached by stairs. Steps also led down to a "lustral basin." This area is called the "Private Quarters" in the *Blue Guide*, but Nanno Marinatos identifies it as a shrine area. Directly across from it are the palace treasuries, in one of which was found the famous Phaistos disk with untranslated hieroglyphic writing in a spiral pattern that we had seen it in the Heraklion museum. Perhaps the disk had been carried by a priestess who descended the steps into the shrine before us.

Our journey continued past farms and olive groves to Agia Triada, a late Minoan "villa" or religious/social/economic center with extensive storerooms and an open court where rituals may have been performed. Agia Triada is only a mile or two from Phaistos, but close to the sea, which glistened in the distance like a turquoise jewel. Here the much-reproduced Agia Triada sarcophagus with detailed paintings of post-Minoan rituals was discovered. On one side, a woman pours a libation into a vessel that stands between two life-size double axes used as a perch by birds. On the other, a bull is tied, waiting to be sacrificed while a woman performs a ritual at an altar crowned by sacred horns.

We found the post-Minoan shrine, a rectangular room about the size of the small chapels that dot the landscape of Greece. It was divided into two square rooms with a long bench, identified as a altar, at the back of the inner room. Here we inaugurated what would become our ritual tradition, placing offerings of small terra-cotta pitchers and tiny hand-sewn triangles filled with sweet-smelling herbs made by the nuns at Paliani on the altar. We added an ancient stone brought from Lake Michigan, jewelry to be blessed, and the small Neolithic Snake Goddess.

The ritual began with the offering of libations: first milk, the nurturing liquid that pours from female breasts, both human and animal; then honey, sweet gift of the bee, reminiscent of the juices that flow from women's sacred place; followed by water, source of life bubbling up from the rocks; and finally, wine, giver of joy, loosener of limbs and spirits, symbolic of women's blood, the blood of birth and renewal. As liquid poured from our hands and settled in to the worn places in the rocks, we returned the gifts of life to the Earth. Our gestures were hesitant and much was left unspoken, but we felt our connection to the ancient women who had made similiar offerings in this very place. Soon the altar stone was wet, sticky, and glistening. Someone noticed a double axe etched onto the front of the altar and outlined it with water. We offered each other honey from a ceramic cup, repeating, "taste the sweetness of life." Robin led us in song. Our ritual ended with a tight embrace, all of us together in a dense circle. Taking care to ground the energy in the earth, we tucked our offerings into crevices or left them for other pilgrims to take home.

During the ritual, one of the women worried that the guards, who were men, were watching us and might try to stop us from performing our ritual. I said that I had never known a ritual to be interrupted by a guard, though once, at Eleusis, a woman guard asked me not to "dirty" the site with the flour I was strewing along the sacred way. We were not interrupted by men—or by women—at Agia Triada or anywhere else on the trip. Indeed, several men appeared along the way to help us, and all the men who observed us, including our busdriver, showed us the greatest respect. This seemed appropriate, and opened me to a deeper understanding of Minoan spirituality, which, while centering on the Goddess, did not exclude the God. I saw that men can accept, and appreciate, and even be present at women's mysteries, as Naomi and I had been present at the men's mystery of the distilling of the rakí. On several occasions during our trip, especially the next day at the Skoteinó cave, I felt the presence of men, just outside our circle of women, to be a great blessing.

MUSIC IN ZAROS

$\mathscr{B}$ack in Zaros, we rested in anticipation of a night of Cretan music and dancing. Because I wanted to share some of the magic that Naomi and I had experienced at the rakí festival, I had asked Kostas, who sings and plays the Cretan lyre, and Giorgos, the young boy who accompanies him on the guitar, to perform for the group at the taverna where Naomi's and my adventure in Zaros had begun. Nikos and Themis, the two young men we had met the previous year, promised that they would ask some of their friends to join us. The group invited a tall, shy, handsome waiter from the other restaurant, and he brought the sweet, round-eyed young woman who was the receptionist at the hotel.

The evening got off to a typical "Greek" start. Kostas, who had played in his regular clothes and without microphones at the rakí party, arrived dressed in his best traditional Cretan black shirt and high black boots, with a three-piece band and amplifiers. I was afraid we might hear a performance packaged for tourists rather than the spirited, spontaneous singing I remembered. And there was another problem. Giannis, the friendly fat man who owns the taverna, had offered to handle the negotiation of the price, but he hadn't done it. Kostas asked me for four times the admittedly low price Giannis had told me was standard. We finally compromised somewhere in between, but I wasn't sure that Kostas was happy. For me, the evening had gotten off on the wrong foot.

My spirits lifted as soon as the music started. The once strange sounds of the Cretan dances had become familiar. I thought back to the night in August when Naomi and Natalie and I were sitting with Nikos while Themis served us dinner. Four men arrived with their instruments and "kefi," the desire to have a good time. I had danced with Nikos that night, and with Andreas, a dignified older man from Anogeia. Though I often have difficulty with dances that have steps—I am most at home with the freeform rock of the late 1960s and early 1970s—Nikos and Andreas were patient with me that night until I caught on.

As soon as Kostas started playing, Nikos pulled me and the others onto the dance floor. He led us all, and with my arm on his shoulder, I danced beside him at the head of the line, unable to hide somewhere in the middle as I usually do. I picked up the steps without thinking and flowed with the spirit all night long. When the band played the zembetiko, the melancholy dance of the Greeks driven from their homes in the cities of Constantinople and Smyrna in 1922, Nikos danced the first solo, arms out, swooping and turning like a bird in flight. I was his audience, joining him on the dance floor, where I stooped and clapped to the rhythm of his movements. Nikos ended his dance by bending down to kiss me. He pulled me up, insisting that I dance my own solo. This was the one dance I had learned fairly well in Lesbos, and I took my place in the center and began to dance, as the Cretan men and American women sat around me on their haunches urging me on with their clapping.

The band played on and on. Wine and rakí flowed. And we danced on and on, now in a circle, now snaking in and out between the tables. There was not a wallflower in the room. Most of us were in our forties, and most of the men were in their twenties, but they told us with their eyes and with words that they thought we were beautiful. Themis' identical twin brother Andreas sang mandinatas, the Cretan songs of longing and rejection, that we had heard for the first time at the rakí festival, after I refused his offer to "get to know each other better." Most of us were sweetly propositioned at least once. Marian, a buxom, heavyset woman in her forties, laughed when she said she told one of the young men that he was the same age as her son. But when she told the story again and again, it was easy to see that she had been flattered by his interest. In the summer, Naomi's ten-year-old daughter Natalie had commented, "The Cretan men like women more than the men at home do." This seemed true. The men had an open appreciation of our femaleness, a playfulness and an gentle insistence that told us they would be honored if one of us said "yes." They made us feel happy to be alive, proud to be women. There were a few kisses and close, slow dances at the end of the evening but, as far as I know, nothing more. In the morning many of us and, I am sure, many of them, were smiling. An elemental sense of the goodness of our sexuality had been affirmed.

BEGINNING HERE

$\mathscr{T}$he next day we got up early to drive back through the mountains to Heraklion and on past Knossos to Archanes. There we would visit the peak shrine on the top of Mount Juctas, the high mountain visible from between the horns of consecration at Knossos. Though I had called the telephone number I had been given many times to confirm our arrival with the guard who had the key to the peak shrine, no one had answered. Still, I took heart in the assurance I had been given that the guard lived in town and was always available. When we got to the new museum, which had discoveries from the palace or cult center at Archanes and from local shrines, I was informed that the guard with the key had returned to his village to vote, and there was no one else on duty. I screamed out, "Then there's no one to take us to the peak shrine," and stormed out of the museum.

My destination was the cafeneion where I had been told the guard always spent his free time. A woman who worked behind the bar and several older men came to my aid, mulling over the situation together and trying to calm the Greek-speaking blonde giant who had appeared in their midst like an angry Goddess. One of the old men finally suggested we consult the mayor. He took me to the local bank where he asked the manager to place the call. The mayor informed me that the missing guard worked for the state, not the village, and therefore the matter was not in his jurisdiction. But, just as I began to erupt again, he said that the archaeologist, a Mrs. Karetsou, was excavating the site as we spoke. He assured me that she would let us in.

Peak shrines were situated near Minoan towns and villages. Mount Juctas would have been a steep climb, but only an hour or two from Archanes, and probably not more than three from Knossos. As little as twenty years ago mountain villagers of all ages and both sexes were used to walking in the mountains with their sheep and goats, and even today Cretans make pilgrimages on saints' days in the summer to the little churches on the tops of high mountains. The walk to Juctas, like the climb to the churches, would have required some effort, but it would not have been difficult except for the very young and the very old.

Our bus wound its way up the side of the mountain on a dirt road, stopping at the entrance to a new stone path that led upward, after about ten minutes, to the top of Mount Juctas. We decided to walk in silence. Giannis, our busdriver, went ahead of us, and when we arrived, he was speaking animatedly with the archaeologist. A few minutes later, he informed me that she was a friend of his, because he had once excavated with her on this site. He said that after some heroic efforts of persuasion on his part, she had reluctantly agreed to speak to us.

Alexandra Karetsou is an attractive woman with a strong, quiet grace. As she stood on the rock outcropping of the peak, it seemed to me that her short sturdy legs were rooted in the mountain itself. Dressed in blue jeans and a lavender T-shirt, wearing sunglasses and an old white straw hat with a scarf covering her hair, she was not dressed like the bare-breasted Mountain Mother Goddess who, in her flared skirt, is pictured rising from the mountain on a famous seal ring. But she had the same power. Behind her was a 360-degree view of agriculturally rich valleys, surrounded by mountains in the distance on three sides, and the sea to the north. A phrase from a song we had sung the day before returned to my mind: "I circle around, I circle around, the boundaries of the Earth."

Professor Karetsou spoke hesitantly and very seriously at first, quoting authorities to back up everything she said. But as she sensed that we understood what she was saying with our bodies and spirits as well as our minds, she began to smile shyly and to speak more freely. She told us that the mountaintop had become a shrine not only because Juctas is the highest peak in the proximity of Knossos and Archanes, but also because in the rock there is a gaping hole, an opening to the depths of Earth. Juctas was visited for more than a thousand years, in the Minoan, post-Minoan, and Greek periods.

The deity worshipped was most definitely the Goddess, and probably in later periods, also the Cretan Zeus. "But the Cretan Zeus," she said conspiratorially, "was a young, unbearded youth. He had nothing to do with that old bearded man with the thunderbolts worshipped by the Greeks." The offerings retrieved from the crevice ranged from simple terra-cotta votives to richly decorated pottery and stone offering tables with inscriptions in Linear A. The pilgrims must have come from all walks of life. Their offerings—images of farm animals and women giving birth, others of arms and legs—suggest that their prayers were for health, wealth, and fertility, not differing much from those a traditional Cretan peasant might make today in a Christian church.

Sensing that we would understand, Alexandra Karetsou told us that when she had excavated small images of women squatting in the birthing position, the male archaeologists, with the exception of the eminent Professor Platon, refused to recognize them for what they were. "So," she said, "when I discussed these images at the archaeological meeting, I had to say, 'Professor Platon has identified them as images of women giving birth.'" At that moment I felt us all connecting as women, and I knew we would tell her about our search for the Goddess.

When she finished, we began to speak about our odyssey. "There are many women like us in America eagerly awaiting the work of women like you," I concluded, wondering what new interpretations might come forth if women archaeologists, instead of laboring to prove the obvious, could write as freely of what they sensed and felt as men have always been able to do.

It was time to approach the crevice. A Greek archaeologist friend told me that though she is not "given to such things," she had a mystical experience while looking into the opening on Juctas. I must have imagined it to be a narrow crack in the rock, because I was suprised to find myself gazing down into a wide deep hole that looked like a steep entrance to a cave. "Did the Minoans descend into the crevice?" I asked. "I don't think so," Alexandra Karetsou clarified. "The workers have been able to descend only with ropes. And it is very dangerous. We have excavated to a depth of thirteen meters. The crevice was filled with votive offerings, and we have not gotten to the bottom yet. We'll probably stop, because of the danger." I asked if we might pour libations into the opening. "Pour anything you want," she replied, "and you can throw in offerings too, if you like."

We poured libations and dropped votive offerings down into the depths. I hurled a small ceramic vase and watched it vanish from sight. Then I remembered the rather gawdy large red brocade sacred heart I had picked up at Paliani while the others were buying lace. I found it in my bag and threw it into the opening in the rocks, asking for the heal-ing of my broken heart. It stuck on a ledge about ten feet down. I wanted it to go all the way to the bottom, so I borrowed a bottle from one of the women and began pouring water on it. I breathed an enor-mous sigh of relief as the force of the water disloged the heart, and it fell into the darkness. I realized that with the winter rains, it would dis-solve into the elements. I sat for some time, looking into the depths. Then I got up and went to one of the highest places, spontaneously raised my arms and began turning, circling around, circling around, the boundaries of the Earth.

SURPASSING
EVERY EXPECTATION

$\mathcal{O}$ur afternoon destination was the Skoteinó cave in the mountains in the area of Pediadas, not far from Heraklion, where in the the spring, I had descended alone into the darkness. That day I had met Christina, a sweet-faced woman in her fifties, who has the round full-breasted, full-bellied body and narrow arms of the Venus of Willendorf, and the tiniest trace of a mustache. The owner of one of the town's two small cafeneions, she had eagerly agreed to cook a special lunch for the group. I asked her to make us stuffed tomatoes with rice and no meat, a Greek specialty.

Though we arrived at Christina's a bit later than expected, the tables were not set. My heart sank. "What else can go wrong?" I wondered. I organized the group to set the tables with the glasses and silverware we found in the dishrack. Christina soon appeared bearing plates of fried potatoes and tzatizki, yogurt and cumcumber dip. The hungry women descended on the food, while I opened the refrigerator and took out beers and cokes. Christina set out tomato and cucumber salads garnished with tiny Cretan olives, and then went back to the kitchen in her house to get the main course. The huge pan full of tiny stuffed grape leaves, stuffed squash blossoms, and the smallest stuffed tomatoes and peppers I had ever seen surpassed every expectation. The group ate greedily, savoring every mouthful. When everyone was sated, there was still a lot left. I suggested that we stop on our way back from the cave to finish the food.

Shortly after we had arrived in the little town of Skoteinó, we were joined by Mr. Nikos, the cave man. Sixty-eight years old, Nikolaos Marakis is a tall, quiet man with thinning whitish hair, a round face, sensitive eyes, and the hint of a scar on his upper lip. He has been exploring the cave since he was a little boy. He worked with the speleologist Paul Faure and with Costis Davaras, the archaeologist who excavated in the 1960s. Now he waits in town for the arrival of the few tourists who make their way to Skoteinó; sometimes in the summer he descends twice a day with them into the cave. With infinite kindness, he guided Naomi and her daughter Natalie and me into the cave, calming Naomi's fears. He waited quietly at a distance while we poured libations and created our ritual. Naomi fell a little bit in love with him that day. For me, Mr. Nikos became the mirror through which I imagined Minoan men—gentle, graceful, helpful, at home in his body, in love with nature, deeply respectful of women. I had explained to Mr. Nikos that the group I would bring in October would probably want to descend into the cave on their own.

When Mr. Nikos arrived to greet us, he won me over with his shy smile and and obvious delight at seeing me again. I didn't have the heart to disappoint him. In the end, I understood that he had appeared to remind me that I don't have to do everything myself. He showed us the path and offered his foot to stand on as we climbed down over slippery rocks. I did not have to worry that someone might fall.

On the way to the cave, I told the group the story of my solitary descent. As I finished, the bus pulled up in front of the little white church above the cave. Mr. Nikos was waiting for us in his three-wheeled open farm vehicle, a sort of Greek go-cart. Our busdriver Giannis decided to come with us into the cave. We went first into the little church of Agia Paraskeví to light candles and say prayers. It seems appropriate that Agia Paraskeví, the patronness of eyesight, is worshipped in the cave, because sight can be understood to include the ability to see in the darkness, and the powers of trance and second sight. Mr. Nikos told us that an earlier church, destroyed by the Turks, had been built near the opening of the cave.

In the enormous room that is the first level of the cave, he pointed out a large rock formation with an image of a mother on one side and a family on the other. I remembered that it was here, below this rock, that Naomi and I had created our sister-bonding ritual, tying three pairs of shiny colored beads together, symbolizing our adoption of each other as family.

The group struggled to focus on the images Mr. Nikos showed us. Our eyes, still adjusting to the semi-darkness, traveled to other mysterious shapes illuminated by the dim light from the opening. We lit our candles and prepared to descend to the second level. Here the path ended, and we had to find our way in and around the cold damp rocks. As the cave grew darker, it would have been easy to slip, but Mr. Nikos waited patiently at every difficult turn, offering a hand, a shoulder, or a foot to lean against.

He guided us to an alcove on the second level, presided over by a tall stalagmite with a clearly discernable face, identified as the Minoan Goddess Vritomartis. Below it was a natural altar, a large, raised, flat surface, and next to it a crevice, a round hole, into which the Minoans dropped their offerings. There, Naomi and I had released the beads we had tied together, affirming that for the rest of our lives we would be sisters. On the floor in front of the altar and in the crevice, the archaeologists found the shards of many terra-cotta offering bowls and libation vessels.

It was almost dark in the small room, so we placed our candles around the altar. I set my little Goddess next to a small ceramic copy of a votive lamp. On her head I placed a silver ring with an openwork design, my thank offering for the gifts the cave had given me in the spring and summer. It fit her like a crown. The others added stones, terra-cotta pots and pitchers, and jewelry. Mr. Nikos and Giannis stood quietly outside the circle while we poured milk and honey to the Goddess Vritomartis and to Skoteiní, the Dark One. Then water and wine. The altar glistened in the candlelight.

Robin, our youngest member, whom I named group nymph, in charge of merrymaking, led us in song. "We all come from the Goddess / And to Her we shall return / Like a drop of rain / Flowing to the ocean." "The Earth is our Mother / We will take care of Her." "The Earth is a circle / She is healing us / We are a circle / We are healing you." Our voices echoed against the walls of the cave. After we closed the circle, Mr. Nikos chose Robin and Cathleen, one fair, willowy, and youthful, the other dark, sturdy, and full-bodied, and asked them to stand one on either side of a stalagmite column. We took their picture as he insisted. But even without photographs, the image would have been etched in our memories because they were perfect icons of the Daughter and the Mother Goddesses. Afterwards, we wedged our offerings into the walls of the cave, threw them into the crevice, or simply left them on the altar. As I heard my silver ring fall deep into the cave, I felt enormous gratitude.

We gathered our things and prepared ourselves for the more strenuous descent to the third and fourth levels. Here the cave was very steep in places and the light grew faint. Mr. Nikos was there to guide us, and Giannis caught one woman who started to slip. I was the first to arrive, elated, at the completely dark fourth level, the oval room with the large solid stalagmite formation in its center, the aniconic image of the Goddess. I immediately sat down with my back against Her, feeling Her power flow into me. Cathleen sat on one side of me and Sue on the other. The others arrived one by one.

When we had all settled down, I said to Mr. Nikos, "We would like to extinguish the candles and sit in the darkness." Without light, the cave was completely dark. After a few seconds Giannis began to talk to Nikos. "Siopí, Silence!" I called out. As we sat quietly in the dark, I "heard" new words to one of the songs we had just sung: "We all come from the Goddess / And to Her we shall return / *From deepest Earth / A circle of rebirth*."

After some time had passed, I sensed that Cathleen was shaking uncontrollably. I took her hand and reached out my other hand to Sue. Cathleen continued to shake. Because I had been meditating on my own pain, asking the rocks to absorb and transform it, I assumed that Cathleen was sobbing. When she did not stop shaking, I broke the silence saying, "We give our pain to the rocks. We ask that it be transformed." A few seconds later, we heard "Siopí, Silence!" echo from the other side of the room.

I started to laugh, and Cathleen joined in. "The busdriver just told me to shut up because I told him to shut up before," I announced to the group. We were all giggling as we lit our candles. Our pain had indeed been transformed. Giannis' words were not an intrusion: they were the stimulation that moved us on. Later Cathleen told me she had not been feeling pain. She had been overpowered by an enormous energy. She said that this sometimes happened to her and she didn't understand what it meant. Sue said that she had felt the energy coming through me to her.

"Oh look! I see a Goddess!" Robin cried out, focusing her flashlight high up on the cave's wall. "Do you see Her! Do you see Her!" she shouted excitedly. "Oh look! Another one!" someone else exclaimed. "And one over here!" "A mother and a daughter!" "An old woman!" "A witch!" And on and on around the room. The darkness had given us second sight.

I led the way back, while Mr. Nikos and Giannis helped those who were unsure of their footing. The climb was strenuous and tested our strength, but we all made it. I was the first to reach the light. Sue and Terry, best friends who had come together on the tour, were next. "I feel like I have been reborn," Sue exclaimed in her lilting Southern accent. "When I was born, my parents wanted a boy. I suffered a lot because of that. Now I'm so glad I'm a girl." "I'm glad you're a girl," I said, as Terry and I embraced her. "I'm so glad you're a girl!" Sue said to Terry and to me, giving us each a hug.

The three of us watched as a procession of women, each with her own candle and coming at her own pace, slowly, appeared out of the darkness. As each one drew near, we cried out, "Oh good! Another girl! Another girl has been born!" This ritual is powerful, because there is not one of us—even those whose parents' wanted a girl when we were born, even those as beautiful as Sue—who has not felt at some point in her life that she would have been more appreciated if she had been a boy. It is hard to imagine how different our lives might have been if we had been born into a culture like the ancient Minoan one that truly rejoiced in our being what we are, girls!

Tired, but renewed, we returned to the mother who would feed and appreciate us, Christina. She and two slight men, her husband and a cousin, were waiting for us. We grabbed our plates and filled them full, helping ourselves to beer and cokes. The radio was playing Greek music, and everyone felt gay. We toasted Christina, and she toasted us. We raised our glasses to Mr. Nikos, and he wished that we all would come back. We laughed and sang and talked about our courage, stuffing ourselves. Our busdriver Giannis, a short, deeply tanned man who wears a white baseball cap to cover his thinning hair, dared us to guess his age. Cathleen, always ready for a challenge and never afraid to make a fool of herself, guessed fifty-seven. Giannis laughed and clicked his glass against Cathleen's, explaining that his bald head made him look far older than his forty-five years. Cathleen's distinctive belly laugh followed as I translated. She gave her trademark "thumbs up" gesture to Giannis, communicating with him in a common language.

When we thought we could eat no more, Christina produced a honey-drenched cake. "They baked cakes to the Queen of Heaven,"[10] I proclaimed, taking a piece and savoring its sweetness. We proposed another toast to the cook. "Was it really good?" Christina asked. When the cake was demolished, I reluctantly announced that we must leave.

Christina said that the drinks from our lunch had been paid for by Mr. Nikos, while the drinks from our dinner were her gift. She then asked us each to pay about half of what I had expected. The group left almost twice as much as she asked. "Each one paid what she wanted to," I said to Christina as I handed her a large wad of bills, probably amounting to more money than she usually makes in a month. "Goodbye, and we'll see you in the spring," I added, embracing her warmly. "Next time you'll have to let me make you something really good," she said with a wide smile.

Christina must have gotten a shock when she counted the money, because, as the bus was about to leave, she handed me a large tupperware bowl filled with golden raisins like the ones we had seen drying in racks along the road to and from Heraklion. "We can't take this," I began. "Take it," Giannis said firmly. Properly admonished, I stammered, "Thank you," to Christina, adding, "we'll eat these on the bus." "Share them with the group," she said, "but I want you to have most of them." We passed the raisins around the bus whenever we were hungry, and left some as offerings in various places, but like the proverbial loaves and fishes, there were always more.

HARVEST HOME

$\mathcal{O}$ur first destination the next day was to have been the cave in Amnissos, a place of pilgrimage in Minoan times and sacred to the Eilitheia, Goddess of childbirth in Greek and Hellenistic times. The key to the gate was kept by the guard at Nirou Hani, a Minoan "villa" or shrine complex where the three large standing double axes on display at the Heraklion museum were found. When we got to Nirou Hani, there was no sign of the likeable, stocky guard who had taken the five of us to the cave the previous year. I sent the group for an early morning swim, hoping he would turn up late.

I questioned the owners of the nearby shops and finally learned that the new guard, a young woman, was having gum surgery and had not appeared at work for several days. I shared the bad news with Giannis who proposed that we visit the archaeological site at Chersonisos, where a young woman was directing the excavation of an early Christian basilica.

Giannis gestured to Cathleen to stop as she started to get on the bus with sandy feet. "He says he just cleaned the bus yesterday," I told her. "She's just like a child," I said to Giannis in Greek. "Yes, she is," he agreed, "but she has a very good heart." So do you, I thought.

When everyone was back on the bus, I expressed my frustration to the group, recalling the Greek phrase, "ti na kano," "what can I do?" I reminded them that the joy we had shared the day before with Christina and Mr. Nikos had been possible because we had been open to unexpected grace. Today we would have make the best of unexpected disappointment.

Chersonisos is one of the overbuilt tourist centers of Crete. Its once peaceful white sand bay is now lined with hotels. The beach was filled with "English lobsters," tourists so glad to be in the Greek sun that they took no care to protect themselves from its damaging and cancer-producing rays. Their willful lack of concern for their pale bodies was painful to me, symptomatic of the lack of concern for the Earth that allows a place like Chersonisos to be built.

Giannis, pleased to be given the opportunity to take charge of fifteen women, set off with a swagger. When we arrived, he was still speaking with the pretty young archaeologist, Vasiliki Sythiakaki. Giannis finally persuaded her to show us the early Christian basilica. Its location on a rocky point jutting out into the turquoise sea was stunning. Possibly this was also the location of a Greek or Roman temple to the Goddess Vritomartis, but the evidence is not conclusive.

At midday we arrived at Malia, a Minoan "palace" built at the edge of the sea, I discovered that I had lost or forgotten the free pass to the site. I had dropped it once at Knossos and a second time at Phaistos. Still, I was fairly certain I had not lost the pass, but had put it inside the guidebook to Phaistos, which I had left in my hotel room. Carol took my "error" in stride and paid the admission for the group out of our emergency funds.

Losing or forgetting the pass made me realize that I was even more tired than I thought. The trip was going very well, but I was still trying to "control" everything. I had not recovered from my loss of sleep on the ferry, and, in addition, I had developed a bad cough in Zaros.[11] I knew I was overextending myself, but because I was the only one who knew Greek, there were very few tasks I could delegate to anyone else. Carol agreed to take responsibility for the pass if I found it. Giannis offered to help with phone calls. Several of the women offered to do little things, like bring me sodas, or rub my shoulders when I felt tired.

I hadn't been certain that we would be able to create a ritual at Malia. But the guards left us alone when we gathered around the kernos stone just inside the main entrance to the "palace" or shrine complex. The kernos stone is a flat circular grey slab about three feet across with thirty-four shallow round indentations around the outside, and two larger and deeper ones in the center, for offerings and libations. We placed the fruits of the earth on the stone: beans, onions, garlic, apples, tomatoes, eggplants, and squash; purchases I had made from a gypsy's truck at Nirou Hani. We thanked the Goddess for the harvest that had provided the wonderful food we had been eating in Crete. Then we named and gave thanks for the spiritual harvest. I thanked the Goddess for the women who had come on the pilgrimage and for the return of the muse that inspires my writing. Others thanked Her for the being able to come on the tour, for the renewal of love, for health, wealth, and happiness. The hot sun beat down on our bodies.

After the ritual, we split up to explore the site. I was with Jana and Karen, who usually sat beside me in the front of the bus, and Cathleen, who had begun to stick to me like glue. We found Sue and Terry, together as usual, inside the "lustral basin." It was a small sunken chamber perhaps eight feet square, several steps lower than the adjoining small rooms. "This was called a bathing room by Sir Arthur Evans, but it has no drain, a technology the Minoans were proficient at constructing," I explained. "Nanno Marinatos thinks that these small rooms, which would also have been dark, were used for initiations."

Soon we were anointing one another with water, proclaiming ourselves Minoan priestesses. Each woman stood in the center of the chamber while water was poured over her head. Then she was told to raise her arms, elbows bent, palms open, like the Goddess in Minoan frescoes and ceramic images, and to turn round and round. The others, forming a protective circle, also raised their arms and turned round and round, leading the initiate in a ritual chant, "I circle around, I circle around the boundaries of the Earth." From our vantage point in the ruined chamber, we looked across the ruins of Malia to the grey and green mountains towering to the south and the clear blue sea to the north. I didn't know what the others felt, but I remember thinking: this seems a bit presumptuous; I don't know if we are ready to become Minoan priestesses. But for six of us at least, and no doubt for some of the others, our initiation was confirmed later in the trip.

PANAGIA IN CHAINS

*T*he next day we set out for the Psychró and Trapeza caves located on the Lasithi plateau high in the mountains of central Crete. I had included a stop at the nunnery of the Panagia Kerá Kardiotissa to break up the long bus ride. I did not anticipate that it too would become a site of revelation.

The convent is nestled among massive tree-covered mountains fashioned of grey rock. Like many holy places in Crete, its church is dedicated to the birth of the Virgin Mary, an aspect of what I call the matrifocal subtext of Christianity, because the major actors in this story are the Mother and Daughter, not the Father and Son. One of the icons in the church depicts Saint Anne lying in bed just having given birth to Mary, who rests in a small cot near her mother's bed. A group of three women prepare a feast in honor of the birth.

The most important icon of the Panagia in this convent is known as "Alyssodemeni," or "Chained." It was stolen and taken to Constantinople, but twice mysteriously returned to the nunnery. The third time it was stolen, it was chained to a column in Constantinople so that it could not return home. This time, it was found, still chained to a green marble column, in the garden of the convent. The icon was placed inside the church with the chain, while the column remained in the garden where it was found, testimony to the miracle.

Inside the small dark church, I waited my turn to kiss the icon. I smiled at Marian, a Southern woman who had been raised on a farm. She had endeared herself to me when I asked her if she was enjoying the tour, and she reponded that she was as "happy as a pig in mud." Approaching the icon, Marian and I found ourselves mesmerized by the Panagia's chain. Marian took it in her hands and gently shook it. I knew that she had recently suffered the loss of love, and I imagined that she was praying to be released from the chains that bound her. "I often pray to find my true love," I confided, "but today I pray simply for 'mental' health, for an end to my suffering which is triggered by feelings of total abandonment. Now I realize that if I could have 'mental' health, it would be enough." We held the chains together, silently repeating our prayers with tears in our eyes. The Virgin's eyes seemed unspeakably sad. We sensed that she too was chained by the forces that had suppressed and bound women and the Earth.

Later, standing alone in the walled garden of the convent, I looked out to the surrounding mountains and felt peace enter my soul. A song came to me. Its tune was familiar, its words new.

> *Mountain Mother, I hear you calling me*
> *Mountain Mother, please hear our cry*
> *Mountain Mother, we have come back to you*
> *Mountain Mother, we hear your sigh.*

The Mother sighs in sadness, but also in relief that we have returned to honor Her once again. I called to Marian and sang to her. Understanding that She needs us as much as we need Her, we held each other in the light and in the embrace of the ancient Mountain Mother.

SOUR MILK

*L*eaving the convent, our bus climbed higher into the mountains, to the Lasithi plateau, a rich and fertile plain surrounded by twenty small villages, framed by high mountains. The highest mountain is Dikte, home to both the Psychró and Trapeza caves.

The cave is called "Psychró," which means bitterly cold, as indeed it must be when the mountains are blanketed with snow. The cave is a well-known tourist destination, both because of its stunning beauty, and because of the legend that Cretan Zeus was born or nurtured there. The Cretan Zeus is not—as Alexandra Karetsou had reminded us—the long-bearded warrior and rapist worshiped as Father on the Greek mainland by the Myceneans and their successors. The Cretan Zeus was honored in his "birth" place; his image was that of an unbearded youth; and it was never forgotten that he was the son of the Mountain Mother. Indeed, the Psychró cave was probably originally sacred to the Mountain Mother, since the earliest offerings were of food and liquid placed in pottery vessels. Bronze offerings of double axes and weapons were left after 1700 B.C.E. The weapons suggest homage to the Son, but the double axes, never pictured in the hands of a God or man, testify that the Mother was not forgotten.

On the twenty minute walk up the mountainside to the mouth of the cave, I fended off many persistent "sons," local men with powerful lamps, who told me that we needed one of them to take us into the cave. But when we got to the tourist pavillion, I was cornered. As I handed our permit for free entrance to the man in the booth, he cried out, "Karolina, do you remember me?" In fact, I did not recognize him, though I well remembered the afternoon that friends and I had spent with him four years earlier. Manolis Petros confirmed that candles are now prohibited inside the cave and convinced me that our flashlights were not strong enough. I reluctantly agreed to let him guide us. It was taking me a long time to catch on: help was continually being offered to me, even when I did not seek it.

Our descent into the deep, cool, stalactite and stalagmite-filled cave was enhanced, or marred, or not affected one way or the other— opinions were mixed—by Manolis' propensity to put a hand on breasts or buttocks as he helped us find our balance on the slippery path. The Psychró cave, much higher in the mountains, was not only colder, but wetter than the one at Skoteinó. At its bottom is a deep lake, its surface covered with a scum that Manolis told us was candle wax. Many offerings had been found in the lake and wedged in the crevices in the small chamber next to it, where it is said that the infant Zeus was fed milk and honey by a goat and a bee.

Because it was crowded in the depths of the cave, Manolis suggested that we create our ritual in the upper cavern to the right of the modern entrance, a place of little interest to tourists. Most of the earliest offerings had been discovered there, he said, as he showed us the place where a stone libation table had been found.

As had become our custom, we set a variety of offerings, jewelry to be blessed, and the now familiar small Snake Goddess from Ierapetra, on a large rock. One of the women led us in a centering ritual, and I taught the Mountain Mother chant to the group. Then we proceeded with libations. The milk Carol poured from a plastic container had soured, and as she made a white circle around the altar, she reminded us that we have drunk sour milk as well as sweet at our mother's breasts. Someone else poured glistening honey over the offerings on the altar, followed by water and wine.

This set the tone for a ritual that evolved, without our having planned it, into the sharing of stories of closeness and understanding, separation and bitterness, between mothers and daughters. For most of us, our relationships with our mothers are tinged with pain. Because our mothers had not been taught to love themselves and other women, they could not teach us to feel pride and self-confidence in our womanhood. Martha Ann, a slight grey-haired woman four times married, who had enjoyed the attentions of Manolis Petros, began. Her mother had given Martha Ann little praise during her life, but just before she died, she said, "You are like a Queen, Martha Ann." "Better late than never,"

Martha Ann said, her voice choking with emotion. Jana fought against her tears as she told us that her mother had always been a great source of support, and had helped pay for her trip to Crete. Yet when Jana played her cello for her mother, she was often disappointed because her mother didn't always seem to pay close attention. One woman spoke of how she became estranged from her daughter, but later reconciled. For another, separation remains in life, while for Carol, it persists after death. On and on and on, we wove our joy and pain into our women's circle. The only one who did not speak was Cathleen, usually an incessant talker. Later when I asked her why she had not spoken, she said, "It was not a choice. I could not speak." To close the ritual we sang again, thanked the Goddess, grounded the power, and walked down the side of the mountain, continuing to share stories.

AMAZING GRACE

After lunch, ten of us hiked to the Trapeza cave near Tzermiado. It was late in the afternoon, and we were all tired. The Trapeza cave, inhabited in the Neolithic period and later used for burials, has two small easily accessible womblike rooms. We climbed first to a low-ceilinged room that just held us, when seated in a circle. Each of us placed her candle on or near the stone in its center. I nestled my little Neolithic Snake Goddess into a crevice in the rock, and we poured libations of milk and honey, water and wine. Our songs included now familiar Goddess chants and the new "Mountain Mother" one. Robin asked if we would join her in singing a slightly modified version of the well-known Protestant hymn, "Amazing Grace." We sang it like this:

> Amazing grace, how sweet the sound,
> that saved a soul like me.
> I once was lost, but now am found,
> was blind, but now I see.
>
> 'Twas grace that brought my heart to heal,
> and grace my fears released.
> 'Twas grace that brought me back to Thee,
> and grace I still receive.
>
> Through many dangers, storms, and scares,
> I have already come.
> 'Twas grace that brought me safe this far,
> and grace will lead me home.
>
> When we've been here ten thousand years,
> bright shining as the sun,

in endless days, we'll sing out praise,
as when we first begun.

When we finished, Marian said with tears in her eyes, that for the first time in her life, the phrase "for ten thousand years" in the familiar Southern hymn took on concrete meaning. She suggested that we continue the ritual by each speaking all the names we knew in our mother-line, ending with the phrase, "and I am proud," which she spoke loudly and decisively. "I am Carol, daughter of Janet, daughter of Lena, daughter of Dora, whose mother came from Germany, my other grandmother is Mary Rita, daughter of Elizabeth whose mother was born in Ireland, *and I am proud!*" And so on around the circle. Someone else wanted to call out the names of women friends and mentors. A cacaphony of female names was spoken. . . . "Judith, Mara, Naomi, Jude, Jane Harrison, Mathilda Joslyn Gage, Ellen, Chris, River, Pat, Rena, Sonia, Nena, Elie, Axiothea, Photeiní, Maria, Eleni, Liz, Melpo," and hundreds more. Perhaps because we had honestly and openly spoken our pain in the morning, our affirmations seemed to take root in the ancient stones. I was not alone in sensing our connection to the Neolithic women who must have sat in a circle as we did, around a fire, remembering ancestors.

I ONCE WAS LOST

$\mathscr{T}$he next morning we visited the church of Panagia Kerá near Kritsa, nestled in the mountains above Agios Nikolaos. It has stunning fourteenth-century frescoes dedicated to the life of Saint Anne, the mother of the Mother of God, and to the life of the Panagia in the south aisle. Here again, as at Kerá Kardiotissa, mother and daughter play the prominent roles in the drama, which is taken from stories recorded in one of the "apocryphal" or noncanonical Gospels. Saint Anne gazes out from the apse, and the story of her conception of Mary in her old age is depicted along the walls. Her husband Joakim does not believe the angels who tell him his wife will bear a child. Anne's birth of her daughter Mary is depicted as at Kardiotissa, with three attending women preparing a feast. Mary is presented at the temple, then betrothed to Joseph. She weeps when he refuses to believe the angel Gabriel's words. She is tested by the priests who prove her innocent. Joseph leading Mary to Bethlehem is a comical old man. Anne and Mary are depicted as stronger and more confident than their husbands. For a moment, we were tempted to believe that here the stories of Demeter and Persephone were preserved in a different form, and that those who saw these frescoes were still able to rejoice in the power of women and in the birth of girls.

But in another part of the church, a fresco depicted a crowned woman, her eyes in trance, feeding a large snake from a small cup. Reminiscent of the Snake Goddess, she is identified as Earth, who must give up the souls of the dead for the Last Judgment. No longer the Goddess who takes all her children back into her womb to await rebirth, Earth now must hand her children over to a male God who will consign some to paradise, others to eternal damnation. Humans no longer honored the Earth as their true home because they had been taught to fear death and judgment. We felt sad. So much had been lost.

Back in the bus, Jane, our down-to-earth Canadian, asked me if I would explain what I meant when I said that North Americans had much to learn from the attitude expressed in the Greek phrase, "ti na kano," meaning "what can I do?" This began a wide-ranging conversation about how Americans believe that we can control everything, that every problem has a solution, that if we only work hard enough we can succeed, and that if we suffer, it is because somehow we have failed. If you don't like your body, you can change it with surgery like Cher. If you start to age, you can exercise like Jane Fonda and have a face-lift. Some day doctors will find a cure for every disease. Perhaps they will even figure out how to freeze us or clone us so that we will never have to die. We don't really have to worry about the mess we are making of the environment or about nuclear catastrophes like Chernobyl, because some day scientists will find a way to clean everything up. And if you don't like the way your personal life is going, therapy can fix it. For problems in your spiritual life, take a course in miracles.

"Living in Greece," I continued, "I have learned that everyone does not think as we do. Greeks do not believe they can control everything. They expect suffering as a part of life. Perhaps we do not want to adopt the extreme fatalism of the Greek peasant, created not only by living close to nature, but also by years of oppression by foreign powers. Some things *can* be changed, but we can learn from the Greeks to be more accepting of the conditions of life: *there is so much that we cannot control.* Wisdom is knowing which things we can change and which things we cannot, having a sense of time and timing, not expecting everything to be as we want it now, not expecting that everything *can* be as we want it *now.*"

"For example, I used to think," I said, hesitating briefly, "that if I didn't have the lover or husband I thought I needed, it was my fault. If only I did enough therapy or the right ritual, I could get what I wanted. Now I believe that finding the right partner has as much to do with luck or fate as will. Therapy can help me to know myself better, to love myself more. But it cannot find me the right mate. Chance and timing play a role." I paused. "But as I stop trying so hard to get the love I used to think I couldn't live without, I realize that love is everywhere. As my mother died, I understood that love does not ever abandon us. And now," I said, looking around the bus, my eyes coming to rest on the intense golden eyes of the redhead sitting across from me, "I know that Jana loves me." I was remembering a restful conversation we had shared in the hotel garden in Zaros, gazing together at the mountains as night fell. "There was a time when I was so intent on finding a husband that I would have said that the kind of love Jana can give me was not important, because it was not the kind of love I thought needed. After all, Jana will go back to America, to her husband. She will not marry me." About that time, the bus arrived at Gournia.

BUT NOW I'M FOUND

*G*ournia, a Minoan village built on a hillside near the Bay of Mirabello, was once an important seaport. Walls of what seemed to be hundreds of houses had been excavated here at the beginning of the century by the American archaeologist, Harriet Boyd Hawes. There is little to distinguish the narrow stepped streets and closely grouped houses of Minoan times from a contemporary mountain village in Crete. As we walked slowly up the hill, we began to sense what it might have been like to live in this village four thousand years ago.

At the crest of the hill is a town center with an open court that may have been a marketplace and a place for rituals. As we read together from the *Blue Guide* about the settlement, I relaxed and let go of my need to be the expert. The others did all the reading, giving my tired throat, still troubled by a racking cough, a much needed rest. Then I distributed more beans, apples, grapes, squash, cucumbers, garlic, onions, and eggplants for our offering on the kernos stone at the other side of the court. My suggestion that we trace a snakelike path across the court was only partially acted upon.

Those who got to the other side first informed the rest of us that the round stone, described in the old *Blue Guide* as an offering table, was identified in the new *Blue Guide* as a stone for animal sacrifice, while the kernos stone with thirty-two indentations for food and liquid, was to to be found to the south and west of it. Beans and other fruits and vegetables in hand, we spread out, searching for a stone that resembled the distinctive round kernos stone at Malia. Finally Cathleen, reading from the new *Blue Guide*, called us all back to a place just behind the round sacrifical altar. As she spoke, Sue ran her hand over the small rectangular stone before her, and announced that it had exactly thirty-two indentations, not evident to the eye, but apparent as she touched them. We were elated to have sought and found the stone, and relieved to have a place to set our offerings.

As we began our ritual, we were interrupted by a stout Greek woman, a guard at the site, who asked what we were doing. She seemed satisfied with my answer that we were offering fruits of the harvest on the ancient stone. During our ritual, we sang "Amazing Grace," which for many of us had come to express our feeling that it was a kind of grace that had brought us here, to Crete, together. Later, a man from Wales stopped one of us and said how moved he had been to hear us sing a "Welsh" song in this place.

At a lull during the ritual, Jana said, "Karolina seems to need a lot of love. I want to affirm that she is loved." I knew she was thinking of what I said on bus, and I felt she had misunderstood. I wanted to say, "Wait a minute, I wasn't asking for anything. I was just stating a fact. I could just as easily have said 'Cathleen loves me, or Karen loves me'." But something stopped me. A voice inside said: *This is a test. Can you accept the love that is being offered to you now?* At that moment Robin stepped forward and said, "I am a priestess. Clasp hands." We obeyed. "I join your souls together," Robin intoned, "for this passage of life." I *can* accept that, I thought, Jana and I will become soul sisters. Jana stood on her tiptoes and gave me a hug.

Our next stop was the tree-sheltered restaurant of the fancy Istron Bay Hotel. While eating, we looked out a deep private bay edged by white sand and framed by soft ochre sandstone cliffs. After lunch, the sea beckoned. "If you dip three times under the water, you will renew your virginity," I said, recalling a ritual several of us had created in Lesbos. "Who wants that?" Patricia, who had been married for twenty-five years, asked skeptically. "It is an ancient custom," I explained. "It was said that the Goddess Hera renewed her virginity each year with her bath in the sea. I don't think this meant literal virginity, but something more like vitality and hope." "I'll take that," Patricia said, diving under the next wave. I followed, musing on all the blessings that had been offered to me on my journey in Crete.

THE DANCE IS
ABOUT TO BEGIN

The next day we drove through the tropical landscape of eastern Crete to the "palace" of Kato Zakros on the southeastern coast. From Ano (or Upper) Zakros, we would hike down a gorge with cave tombs, the trail ending at the sea at Kato (or Lower) Zakros. The gorge is rocky and wild, the trail not always well marked. Still trying to let go of control, I let others find the path. Several times along the way, we stopped to sing to the lovely mountains on either side of the river-cut gorge. It was a mildly strenuous hike, and I was tired when we came to the end of the trail.

Though some went immediately to the archaeological site, Jana and I proceeded to the first of the several small tavernas in front of the sandy beach. As we sipped cold Amstel beer, I began to realize how exhausted I was. I had been wanting to speak to someone about losing control in my therapy group just before the trip began. The words poured out. I told Jana what happened and how scared I had been. "I have an article one of my therapists wrote," I continued. "It says that part of the healing process is losing control, as you give up old fixed beliefs that have not served you well in life. I feel like I have been changing my beliefs all summer," I said proudly. "I hope I do not have to go through a complete breakdown to get better." "I know what you mean about control," Jana said. "When I play my cello in a quartet or an orchestra, I feel that I have to get every note right. I live my life that way too. Sometimes I am so tired, that I think I don't even want to play the cello any more." "Maybe you should take a break from playing," I suggested. "I have just gone through a period where I scarcely wrote at all for three years. Since the night I expressed my anger at Aphrodite, writing has been flowing out of me. A rest can be good." "Maybe so," Jana replied, "but I'd be scared to do that." "I'm scared of breaking down," I said. "Do you think I will have to?" "Probably so," Jana said, pausing and looking into my eyes, "but maybe it won't be as bad as you think it will be."

Our conversation was interrupted by Giannis and Cathleen who joined us for lunch. Our mood changed immediately. My attention was drawn to a larger than life-size image of the Minoan Snake Goddess painted on the outside wall of the restaurant. I learned that the artist was a dark-haired, dark-skinned man sitting under the painting. "Did you have a feeling for the Goddess when you painted that?" I asked him in Greek. "Not really," he replied in English with a look of utter disdain. "They asked me to paint it, and I did it. That's all." "That dude really had attitude," Cathleen said laughing, when I returned to the table. "Cathleen, you do have a way of putting things," I replied. "A dude with a 'tude," she repeated, giving me the thumbs up gesture, and basking in the affirmation. "I think I'll call his friend, the young Greek waiter with the hairdo, 'John Revolta.'" Jana and I burst into uncontrollable laughter. All through lunch, which took a long time in coming, we giggled about the "dude with a 'tude," who pranced around the restaurant in his short cutoffs, helping "John Revolta." "The dude is not Greek," Cathleen observed. "He is a long long way from home."

After lunch, Giannis went to take a nap in the bus and Cathleen disappeared. Jana and I changed into our suits for a swim. We were joined by a number of others in the healing waters of the sea. The water was refreshing, but I was even more exhausted when we emerged. Several of us set out together for the archaeological site, which, other group members had informed us, was locked. The fence, they said, was easy to climb over.

Once inside, I felt overwhelmingly tired, too tired to go on with the others. As we passed a stone bench to the north and west of the open court, I lay down and closed my eyes. I don't know if I actually slept, but when I opened my eyes, I was in trance: I had awoken to a different reality. I could see the air vibrating, and as I looked to the north up the hill toward the ruins of the Minoan village, I felt I could almost see women moving up and down the stepped paths. My gaze fixed on the village, I watched the movements of women I could not quite see with my eyes. After a while, Cathleen, whose constant talking can sometimes be annoying, came up to me. I didn't want to engage in conversation, so I said to her, "If you sit very quietly, you will see women walking in the village." She sat silently beside me, nodding and smiling broadly when I asked her if she saw what I saw.

After a bit, I moved and sat facing south, at the edge of the central court which was an open rectangular area about one hundred feet by forty feet, surrounded by the remains of sacred buildings. I could still feel the vibrations of the air, and as I looked across the court, I felt a sense of anticipation. "The dance is about to begin," I said to Cathleen when she joined me. She nodded, still smiling. It was about an hour before sunset and the ancient stones were bathed in the last light of day. Jana and Patricia sat talking in the ruins of the central shrine room, while six or seven others leaned over the ancient cistern, watching turtles and turtle babies dive into the water. The women's voices and laughter had a timeless quality. "This was not a palace," I whispered to Cathleen, "it was the community center. It feels as if a dance is about to begin," I repeated.

All of a sudden Cathleen stood and exclaimed, "I see the path of the dance rising up in the court. It looks like the processional pathways we saw at Knossos, Phaistos, and Malia. Do you see it?" Something moved me to the court, where slowly, slowly, my arms raised, bent at the elbows, palms facing forward, I wove my way back and forth across the court, tracing the path of an ancient ritual dance. As I neared the center of the court, it was difficult to keep my footing. Stopping exactly in the center, I turned and faced Cathleen, seated across from me at the end of the court, watching. I gazed at her solemnly, my arms still raised, sending energy through my palms. She slowly raised her arms in greeting. I turned and continued tracing the snakelike path. When I got to the far side of the court, I stopped and turned to greet Cathleen and Robin who had joined her. "The path you walked was exactly the path I saw," Cathleen cried out in astonishment. "You were meant to stop as you did in the center." "It was an ancient path," I replied solemnly, walking slowly back toward the center of the court to embrace Cathleen who met me there.

Robin got up and ran to a spot on the west side of the court, near the center. "I feel that there was an altar or a sacred space here," she said, testing the area with her open palms, trying to sense what it was that had drawn her. "It was near here that I almost stumbled," I said to Cathleen, "as if I felt an energy field too." Jana and Patricia came in from the northwest entrance to the court. Jana leading, with her arms up, palms forward as mine had been, traced another path, with the same slow rhythm I had found. Jana and I met in the center of the court, while Carol, Patricia, Cathleen, and Robin stood in a circle around us, one in each of the four directions.

I turned and walked slowly toward Jana, pausing when our palms came close enough to feel the energy pulsing between us. We stood motionless for some time, and then slowly approached each other, first touching palms, and then kissing each other softly. We sensed that we were meant to share this blessing with the others. Slowly turning, one of us approached the woman in the west, while the other approached the woman in the east, sensing the energy, then touching palms and kissing. We turned back and to the center, repeating the our gestures until we had each greeted all of the other women. As we turned again to face each other, I whispered, "I feel we were called to this dance. This was an initiation." Jana nodded.

It was getting dark by then, so we wove our way back to the gate and climbed over the fence. We returned to the beach, where the rest of the group was sitting in circle of chairs, waiting for us. We told them our story, and then went to liberate the bottle of rakí the busdriver had brought for just such an occasion, from its place by his seat on the bus. We passed it around, drinking deeply as if the rakí might somehow ground the tremendous energy we felt.

MOCHLOS MOTHER

$\mathcal{W}$e awoke early the next morning to drive to Mochlos, a quiet fishing village with several tavernas nestled around a small harbor. At a distance of about five hundred feet, an easy swim in the buoyant placid sea, is Mochlos Island, once attached to the mainland by a peninsula. Minoan ruins are easily visible from shore, spreading out on both sides of a tiny whitewashed church. Tombs had been cut into the grey striated rocks near the top of the island. As the bus navigated the curves of the narrow road that descended to the sea, memories flooded my mind. I thought of the peace I had found in Mochlos and of the many friends I had made there. When I called my favorite taverna the night before to order fish for the group, the owner, Giorgos, recognized my voice before I even said my name.

I had first visited Mochlos in the spring while researching the tour. I planned to look at the site, have lunch, and move on. But it was so beautiful, the fish I had for lunch were so good, and I was so tired that I decided to spend the night. The next day I was still tired, and it threatened to rain on and off all day, so I spent a second night. As I looked across the sea to the tiny island, the plans for the pilgrimage took shape in my mind.

When I returned in June with my friend Ellen, she took charge as usual. "This is where you and Naomi should come for your summer vacation," she said decisively. Seeing Maria and Giorgos sitting on their front porch, she introduced herself, and inquired about their rooms-to-rent. Thanks to Ellen, Naomi and I and her daughter Natalie did spend two wonderful weeks in Mochlos in August, and Maria and I became friends.

Our day in Mochlos was to be a day of rest, with no program. No one needed the rest more than I did. I was still coughing incessantly despite the various herbal remedies given to me by group members. The many responsibilities of leading the trip were still wearing on me. Not to mention the experience at Zakros. After we straightened out the rooms (not an easy task because of the vagueness of the hotel owner), we headed for the sea. The others wanted to explore the island, but I didn't have the energy and swam back to shore.

I saw my friend Efsevia, known to one and all as "Yiayiá," meaning "Grandmother," sitting at a table by the door of the taverna run by her oldest daughter's family. Efsevia has clear, light blue eyes and an elfin smile. Despite many wrinkles, her face is beautiful. Her hair was as yellow as wheat until she was in her seventies. Now eighty-five, she plaits it in two thin braids that crown her head under her black scarf. She wears the black dress of Cretan widows, always with a black and white pinstriped apron, and walks assisted by a simple handcarved cane. When I look into her eyes I cannot help but think that in her youth she could have been a model for one of Titian's paintings. Her face, for me, is a clear reminder of the centuries of Venetian occupation of Crete.

I was thrilled to see Yiayiá, because when I said goodbye to her in August, she said that she would be in the upper village in October, and not to expect to see her next year. However, she had gotten out of her bed, where she had spent eight days sick, to come down to Mochlos with her family to vote. I counted myself lucky. She embraced me warmly, and I sat with my arm around her as she again told me the stories of her life. The pictures Patricia took that day show how tired I was, and catch me at an awkward angle. And yet, as a friend said, they are beautiful because they capture the joy, pain, understanding, and deep love between two women of different generations and very different cultures.

Yiayiá begins every conversation by saying, "I don't know how to write. I couldn't go to school. I don't know anything." To which I always reply, "You know so many things that I don't know." Though she is much loved by everyone, I don't believe many people listen to Efsevia's stories. She has a need to speak of her difficult life. As we sat, a group formed around us, and I translated.

Efsevia was born to a poor family in Sfaka, the mountain village above Mochlos. Her mother died when she was eight years old, leaving her with three younger sisters to take care of. After her father remarried, her stepmother had four more girls and handed them on to Efsevia to raise. There was no time for school. When she was sixteen, a much older man, who had been fighting the war in Asia Minor for six years, came to her father and offered to marry her. She said she was too young. Her father said that because he had eight daughters, and little money for dowries, he couldn't afford to refuse any proposal. Neither Efsevia nor her husband inherited a house from their families, so her husband built their house in Sfaka rock by rock. Now she frets that none of her grandchildren is interested in living there. Her husband was a good man, and in time she came to respect him. She had four daughters. Two of them got sick while she was recovering from giving birth to the third, and one died. The German occupation came, and then the civil war. Times were very hard. There was little food. She struggled all her life working in the fields, tending the animals, spinning, weaving, sewing, preparing food for storage, cooking, and raising the girls. Her husband worked hard too, but her work never ended. Speaking so long seemed to tire her and she said she wanted to rest. She gave me a hug and started up the stairs to her bedroom above her oldest daughter's taverna.

We went on to the other taverna to taste the fish Giorgos had bought for us. Not the little fish I well remembered from spring and summer, but a several-foot-long fish that migrates past Crete in early October. The fish was prepared by Giorgos' mother, Maritsa, a talented cook. It was served with a tangy garlic mayonnaise sauce, fried potatoes, Greek salad, and tiny Cretan olives.

After lunch, I went to my room to rest and didn't awake until dark. When I had showered and dressed, I went back to Yiayiá. An even larger group gathered around. This time the women asked Yiayiá questions. I translated, and she answered. Martha Ann, ever the Pollyanna, asked Yiayiá where the joy had been in her life. Yiayiá seemed not to understand. "Didn't you dance? Didn't you go to panigiris, religious festivals?" I prodded. "When did I have time to learn to dance?" was her reply. "I went to church on Sunday, and then I came home and took the goats up into the mountains. When did I have time for festivals?" "But you must have had some joy," Martha Ann insisted. Efsevia thought for a while and then said, "Yes, now I remember. One night two German soldiers came to our door and asked for food. They came in, and we fed them. We drank wine, and we laughed. They stayed a long time." Someone asked how she could have enjoyed an evening with Nazi soldiers. "Are

all the fingers on your hand the same?" she responded. "There are good and bad people in every group. The German leader was at fault, not those young boys."

The whole time she spoke, I sheltered Yiayiá with my arm, and tightly clasped her hand. I could feel how deeply tired she was. From time to time, I could sense her slipping away. She is ready to die, I thought. I don't think she will make it through the cold winter. When Yiayiá excused herself to go up to sleep, I broke into tears. "What's wrong?" Jana asked, taking her turn to comfort me. "I can feel Yiayiá dying," I said. "I don't think I'll see her again. I wanted to tell her not to go, but I could feel how tired she is. I think she is ready." "It's very sad," Jana replied. "But you've given her a lovely day, a day she'll remember. Did you see how her face lit up when we took her picture? She loved being the center of so much attention."

I cried and cried. For the sadness in Yiayiá's life, for the sadness in women's lives, for the sadness in my life. "Yiayiá has such spirit and such strength," Jana said. "She is a real inspiration. Do you know what a special thing you have done in introducing her to us?" "I am so tired," I said. "I know you are," Jana replied, "But you are doing a wonderful job." We sat for a few moments staring out to sea, and then we went to join the group for dinner.

As we left Mochlos the next morning Cathleen read us a poem she had written before falling asleep. It expressed the sense we all had that in Yiayiá was one of the faces of the ancient Goddess:

> *Mochlos Mother*
> *I hear you calling me*
> *Ancient Mother*
> *Please hear my cry*
> *Mochlos Mother*
> *I have come back to you*
> *Ancient Mother*
> *I hear your sigh.*[12]

A DIFFICULT PASSAGE

*A*s our bus began the climb back up the mountain the next day, I shared a conversation I had with Robin at dinner. "One of the things I worried about when I began to plan this trip was that the group would explode," I began. "In the years I taught in Lesbos, it happened every time. For each group, it was a different issue. I think the real reason was that the women were having a good time and sharing deeply with each other. When they thought of going home to a job they didn't like, or to a partner that wasn't as much fun as the women on the tour, or simply to the stress of life in the United States, they panicked. They tried to destroy the feeling in the group so that it would be easier to return home. When I shared this with Robin, she made a good suggestion. 'Why don't you share your fears and your analysis with the group,' she said. 'The unconscious likes to work in secret. When you expose it to the light of day, it cannot continue.' So, I have decided to share my fear with you, in the hopes that no one will feel the need to destroy what we have created on this trip."

Our destination was Kato Symi, where the guard would be meeting us at the town's only taverna. The road up the mountain was narrow, our bus large, and the curves in the road torturous. I was worried because the guard had told me that he didn't believe our bus would be able to make it up the six-kilometer-long dirt road that wound up from the town to the archaeological site. I urged the group to pray that the bus could make it. I hated to think of our coming such a long way and not being able to see the sacred place. Naomi and Natalie and a young German girl, Lena, and I had driven up the road in our rented Fiat Panda without difficulty in the summer. But we had found the gate locked, the high barbed wire fence impenetrable. I had thought maybe it would be too difficult to bring the group. Naomi insisted that Kato Symi was so beautiful, it was worth any effort to get there. I was elated when, after many phone calls and inquiries, I finally discovered that a guard who lived at some distance from Kato Symi would unlock the gate for us. Now I was afraid we might be disappointed again.

When we reached Kato Symi, our bus could barely navigate the narrow tree-lined streets of the village. The guard, a small rough-looking Cretan with a very big mustache, was waiting for us. He lost no time in informing Giannis that our large bus would never make it up the sandy dirt road with its hairpin curves. I was distraught. Several women in the back of the bus were upset and afraid. We decided to park the bus and retreat to the town's only taverna to discuss the situation. The taverna was filled with the soothing sound of running water, flowing down in channels along the side of the road from the cold spring that emerges near the site of the ancient temple.

While I attempted to calm the group (not feeling particularly calm myself), Giannis and the guard worked out a solution. Two brown-haired pudgy brothers, each with his own farm pickup truck, were having lunch in the taverna. If we paid them enough, they would take us to the site and wait for us. While negotiating a price, I noticed that their food looked delicious. "Do you think we could eat here too," I asked Giannis, "I don't think the tavernas by the sea in Myrtos are very good." "Why not?" he replied. A few minutes later the owner of the taverna pulled half of a freshly slaughtered lamb out of the refrigerator, and suggested that he and his wife would cook it into a stew while we went up the mountain. All problems resolved, we piled into the trucks and set off.

The archaeological site at Kato Symi reminds me of Delphi. High up in the mountains, it is not a peak shrine. Wooded mountains tower above, a nearby spring gives birth to gurgling water, a cave is visible in the sheer rockface to the north, a large boulder, like the one identified with the prophetess at Delphi, stands to one side of the ruins, while the aquamarine sea shimmers below the trees to the south. The site had a continuity of worship for close to two and a half thousand years, from Minoan times until the triumph of Christendom. Worship of the Minoan Goddess and the young God was gradually transformed into worship of Aphrodite and Hermes of the Tree. An ancient plane tree, its trunk open and scarred by a fire said to have been set by the Turks, yet miraculously still living, dominates the site.

My own history at Kato Symi echoed that of the deeply scarred tree. When I had come to Kato Symi four years earlier, I was in the early stages of the anger and despair caused by the ending of my love affair with Nikos. I could not open myself to the transforming power of the Goddess that day, though I did wedge a votive ceramic pot into a crevice in the large boulder, asking that Nikos be returned to me. Miraculously, or so it seemed to me, he had been returned to me over the summer, free of the drugs that had almost taken his life. We were slowly beginning to develop a friendship on the far side of death and had become lovers again just before I left for Crete. I wanted to see if my votive offering was still hidden in the rock.

I also hoped to find evidence of the pilgrimage that Naomi and I had made in the summer. Frustrated in our unsuccessful attempt to scale the fence, we had thrown our votive offerings, pairs of shiny plastic worry beads, mine golden, hers clear blue, bearing hopes for healing and the renewal of love, over the fence near the boulder. Our disappointment dissolved in laughter when eleven-year-old Lena filled her new baseball cap at the spring and doused us with very cold water in the heat of a very hot day.

MANY BLESSINGS

*W*hen we arrived at Kato Symi, I suggested that we explore the site separately, cleanse ourselves in the water flowing from the spring, and then gather around the tree for the ritual reading of Sappho's poetry that we had planned. I went immediately to the boulder, scratching my legs on the thistles that had grown over what once might have been a path. Cathleen followed me. I looked in several cracks in the rock, but did not see my ceramic vase. Then my eyes landed on Naomi's blue beads on the ground near the fence. I picked them up and hurled them as far back as I could, into the largest crevice in the rock. "Here are your gold beads," Cathleen said a few minutes later, casting them into the opening where they landed on top of Naomi's. "It is appropriate that our beads landed together," I said to Cathleen, "because Naomi and I created a sister-bonding ritual with beads like this a few days after our visit here." We were standing quietly by the rock, gazing up at the mountains, when Cathleen began to shake. "I see three women in the cave," she began. "They are wearing long dresses, and they seem to be greeting us." I could not see them, but I felt their presence.

Cathleen and I were among the last to return to the shade of the tree. When we arrived, I saw that the others had already created an altar on the table that someone, probably the archaeologists, had made by wedging a thick plank, supported by stones, against the concave shell of the tree trunk. I added my Goddess and a small ceramic votive pitcher to the plethora of gifts already in and around the tree. I took off my necklaces, draped one over the Goddess, and set the others on the plank to be blessed. Then I hurried over to the stream to wash my hot and grimy face in the cool, healing water.

The group was gathered in a circle around the tree. We poured out milk and honey, then water and wine. Robin led us in song. I opened the ritual by reciting the one Sappho poem I had committed to memory. With a minor change, it provided a perfect beginning.

> *You know the place: then*
> *[Come to us in Crete]*
> *waiting where the grove is*
> *pleasantest, by precincts*
>
> *sacred to you; incense*
> *smokes on the altar, cold*
> *streams mumur through the*
>
> *apple branches, a young*
> *rose thicket shades the ground*
> *and quivering leaves pour*
>
> *down deep sleep; in meadows*
> *where horses have grown sleek*
> *among spring flowers, dill*
>
> *scents the air. Queen! Cyprian!*
> *Fill our gold cups with love*
> *stirred into clear nectar.*[13]

The imagery of the poem evoked the place where we were waiting for the Goddess and She was waiting for us.

I suggested that we each pour a libation of wine mixed with water from the gold-colored earthenware pitcher Marian had provided, before reading our poems. Some of us had choosen a favorite. Others had followed Patricia's suggestion that we open the book three times and read the poem that "chose" us. Patricia, who had fallen head over heels in love with the sheep and goats of Crete and who also had two lovely daughters she doted upon, read the poem that had come up when she opened the book:

> *You are the herdsman of evening*
>
> *Hesperus, you herd*
> *homeward whatever*
> *Dawn's light dispersed*

You herd sheep—herd
goats—herd children
home to their mothers.

Jana, definitely one of the sensualists of the group, chose a poem that
began:

I confess

I love that
which caresses
me.

"Others have criticized that part of me," Jana said when she finished.
"But I affirm it." When it came my turn, I said, "I am going to be greedy.
I chose one poem, and then one chose me. I want to read them both."
The first was a thanksgiving offering for the return of the muse I
thought had deserted me for good, but over the summer came back:

It is the Muses

Who have caused me
to be honored: they

taught me their craft.

The one that chose me represented a hope I would have been hesitant
to voice:

Hymen Hymenaon!

Raise the rafters! Hoist
them higher! Here comes
a bridegroom taller
that Ares!

Hymen
Hymenaon!

He towers
above tall men as

poets of Lesbos
over all others!

Sing Hymen
O Hymenaon

Each woman found a poem that seemed to suit her perfectly. The spirit of Aphrodite so infuses all of Sappho's poems that I belatedly understood that it was not chance that led me to suggest we read Sappho that day. "I thought you consciously recognized the connection between Kato Symi, Aphrodite, and Sappho," Jana said later. "It's an obvious one," I said, "but I was so tired yesterday, I really hadn't given it any thought."

As we came to the close of our ritual, our three male helpers were fidgeting. So we quickly concluded, and piled back into the trucks for the bumpy trip back down the hill. A long table was already set for us when we arrived at the taverna. Soon we were assuaging our hunger with sweet young lamb stewed in tomato sauce, potatoes, salad, tiny black olives, hard Cretan dry bread or paximadia, and local apricot-colored wine. Our host, a tall, graceful, grey-haired man, who appeared to be in his fifties, took out his violin and began to play Cretan mountain songs. His wife, a round-faced simple village woman, gazed at her husband with deep love and admiration as he played.

After a while, Karen, who had been out of sorts and was fasting to cleanse herself, asked if she might play. She treated us first to a fast American country jig, a counterpart to the Cretan dance tunes played by our host. Then she began to play a European violin solo so beautifully that it seemed as if we had entered into a dream.

It had been a long day already, but we still had the early Minoan settlement at Myrtos on our schedule. The bus wound its way back down the hill to the place where two settlements at Myrtos were built on the tops of hills overlooking the sea. Though we were tired, the fifteen minute hike up the hill was easy enough. The view of the coastline and the sparkling sea from the small settlement of closely grouped houses of equal size, was spectacular. I reminded the group that this site, called Phournou Korifi, was the one that classicist Lucy Goodison said demonstrated the communal, egalitarian social structure of the early Minoan period.[14]

Naomi and I thought that we had found the shrine with a low altar bench where the mysterious, long-necked, square-bodied Goddess holding a pitcher was found. But I didn't locate it easily this time. We found several possibilities, disagreeing as to which was the most probable. Patricia took off her necklace, a mauve crystal with a turquoise stone inserted into its gold band, and held it over each of the three "benches," asking, "Are you the Minoan shrine?" In two places the necklace moved in the "no" direction, while in the third, it gave a definite "yes." Though some of us were skeptical, there was no time to disagree. I set my Goddess on the altar, and we created a simple ritual, aware that Giannis was anxious to start back before dark.

Those of us who got down the hill first could not resist the water. So, without going back to the bus for our suits, we slipped naked into the sea. Most of the others joined us. Knowing that the busdriver was waiting, we laughed like little girls who were getting away with something behind their parents' back. Those who hadn't done so at Istron Bay renewed their virginity, and some of us took a few extra dips for good measure. The sun was going down as we splashed and played. As I started to herd the group back to the bus, someone called out "five more minutes," and I dove back in.

The sun set as we crossed the isthmus of the island. We still had a long way to go before arriving back in Heraklion. The next morning we would leave for Anogeia where we would spend our last night in Crete. It was hard to believe that our trip was almost over.

A BRILLIANT
SUGGESTION

I awoke early the next morning. After breakfast, Marian and I decided to make one last visit to the old market area of Heraklion. It was all hustle and bustle as purveyors of herbs and spices, fresh meat and fish, Cretan wedding breads in the shape of wreaths, honey, olives, rakí, leather slippers, shoes, embroidered tablecloths, videocassettes, knives, screwdrivers, and just about everything else, hawked their wares. There was a feeling of excitement in the air. On the way back to the hotel I saw sets of beads like the ones Naomi and Natalie and I had used as votive offerings in the summer. On impulse, I bought a golden pair and another with sparkles of silver, pink, and blue.

We left Heraklion to climb again into the Psiloritis mountains. Our destination was the Idean cave. The Kamares cave, visible from Phaistos, is on the other side of the same mountain. Part way up, we stopped in the village of Tylissos, where three Minoan "villas" had been excavated.

We went first to the little cafeneion next to the site, run by a family of women. While we waited in the courtyard of the whitewashed house to use the bathroom, we noticed several old pithos jars and an outdoor oven, with lunch stewing inside it. The youngest of the women called several of us over to a small room to look at the woven cloths and carpets she had for sale. Some of them were obviously mass-produced for the tourist trade, but eventually she produced several small well-worn handmade rag rugs and a green and white plaid hand-loomed tablecloth. Cathleen bought the tablecloth, while Jana chose a small piece of a rag rug that she said she would put on her altar at home.

The site at Tylissos was bathed in a soft light, and the stone ruins of the Minoan houses seemed to be part of the surrounding agricultural village. The goat tethered to a tree just outside the fence could have belonged to the owners of the Minoan settlement. I remembered an article I had read comparing traditional Cretan farmhouses to the so-called Minoan "villas." The author argued that the size of the houses does not necessarily indicate the great wealth that the archaeologists imagined. She had seen a poor family living in a large stone house, built by hand over several generations. One prosperous, but by no means wealthy, farm family had fifty large pithos jars in its basement for the storage of the staples of a peasant diet: grain, olive oil, cheese, olives, and wine.[15]

I reminded the group that this was the place where three enormous bronze cauldrons, on display in the Heraklion museum, had been discovered. When we read in the guidebook that jars of paint were found near the cauldrons, Patricia made a brilliant suggestion. "I see these houses as the residences and workshops of an extended family engaged in dying of cloth. Those large cauldrons are too big for food, but they are about the same size as the cauldrons I saw used for coloring cloth in India. The 'paints' found near the cauldrons could have been the dye. This area is noted today for its weaving. Might it not have been so in Minoan times as well? Minoan women's lives probably weren't so different from the lives of the women we met next door." Patricia's idea felt deeply satisfying. The ancient stones had begun to speak to us.

GIVEAWAY

$\mathcal{W}$e had a long journey through the mountains ahead of us to the Idean cave. As the mountains grew steeper and steeper, I told the group about an old woman I had picked up along the road from Tylissos to Anogeia. She had come down to go the the doctor and had missed her bus back. To make conversation, I asked about her children and grand-children. "I don't have anyone," she said. "The Germans burned our vil-lage during the war and killed most of the young men. After the war I had nothing. No home, no dowry, no one to marry me. I am all alone now." "The Cretans who lived in these mountains resisted the Nazis throughout the war. There was a great deal of suffering. In Anogeia you will see many old women who never married," I said with a sense of sadness.

The group was silent as we continued to climb through narrow moun-tain passes, ascending higher. Just before we reached Anogeia, we came to a fork in the road marked by a sign pointing the way to Mount Ida. From here it would be twenty-one more kilometers before we reached the Idean cave. I recalled how difficult it had been driving my rented Fiat Panda over the unpaved, rocky, last six kilometers of the road. When I had finally reached the cave in early May, its wide entrance was com-pletely blocked by snow.

The Idean cave is on the tallest mountain in Crete. Like the Psychró cave, it was known as the birthplace of the Minoan Zeus whose worship continued there into Greek times. As at Psychró, the earliest offerings brought to the cave must have been dedicated to the Mountain Mother. Just below the cave is the Nida plateau, which was green and dotted with some eight thousand sheep in the spring, the tinkle of their differ-ently pitched bells creating a haunting melody. On the edge of the plain is a taverna where we would have lunch. As we came up to the plain, I saw that it was dry and brown. Later, I would hear that the shepherds were worried, because by this time of year the winter rains that turn the plain green again should have begun. I wondered if the Minoans prayed to the Mountain Mother for rain and snow at summer's end, and if they thanked her for the melting of the snow in the spring when they drove their sheep back out to the plain. The bus pulled up in front of the taverna, and I remembered that we would have a twenty-minute walk up the mountain to the cave.

It was cold on Mount Ida, so we put on our sweaters. The walk up the mountain rested our active minds, and the exertion enlivened our bodies. We had begun to understand that walking was an important part of the journey to the sacred place, and that the surrounding mountains were as holy as the cave that was our destination.

Jana and I were among the first to reach the cave. I was elated to see it without snow. Narrow train tracks, used by the excavators to bring dirt up from the cave, marked the approach to the enormous mouth. Wide steps descending to a platform at the bottom of the cave took the mystery out of what would otherwise have been a steep climb down. The cave opens out on either side of the platform to two large rooms, both well-lit from the cave's opening. "This is more of a cavern than a cave," Jana commented as we looked around. Droppings on the platform showed us that the cave was home to many birds, and we saw one fly into a crevice high above us. I reminded Jana that for the Minoans the appearance of a bird during a ritual was understood as an epiphany of the Goddess. We recalled the three tiny terra-cotta columns with black birds resting on top of them that we had seen in the museum in Heraklion. Together, Jana and I found a large rock in the deeper chamber that seemed right for the giveaway and goodbye rituals we had planned.

After listening to the guard talk about the Cretan Zeus, we created an altar to his Mother on the rock we had found. Most of the group had fallen in love with my little Goddess from Ierapetra. Giannis, who lives near Knossos, had gone back to the tourist shop where I found her, to buy ten more. We found eleven niches in the rock for our eleven Goddesses, draped them with our jewelry, set our offerings beside them, and wedged our candles into the crevices. I put a ceramic pitcher next to my Goddess, removed my necklaces, and arranged them on the rocks. I remembered the worry beads I had bought in the morning, and added them to the little scene I had created. It was a bit like playing dollhouse. And it looked so beautiful when we were done. Once again, I had the feeling that the Goddesses liked company. They seemed so sweet together.

We poured our libations, milk, both sweet and sour, glistening honey, water, and wine. The ritual that evolved next was totally unplanned, and I cannot remember how it began. What I do remember is that soon we were calling out all the criticisms that had been spoken to us as children. "You're too fat." "You're too skinny." "You're too short." "You're too tall." "You're too smart." "You're too dumb." "You're too goody-goody." "You are bad." "You're wrong." "You're no good at that." "You're fat, fat, fat, tall, tall, tall, skinny, skinny, skinny, dumb, dumb, dumb, smart, smart, smart." "You are wrong." After each criticism, the group repeated a favorite childhood response, "Nah-Nah-Na-Nah-Nah. Nah-Nah-Na-Nah-Nah." The energy built and built as we exorcised the labels that had crushed our spirits. "You cry too much." "Nah-Nah-Na-Nah-Nah." "You're too sensitive." "Nah-Nah-Na-Nah-Nah." We went on and on, reclaiming the girls we had been, affirming the women we are, the women we can become. As a result of our pilgrimage we were shedding the legacy of self-hatred we had inherited from our culture. This ritual confirmed the changes that were taking place within us.

We had planned a "giveaway," in which each of us would give, and each of us receive, a gift. Remembering the blue ribbon I had received at Paliani and feeling grateful for the protection I had received during our journey, I had decided that my gift would be a blue "eye." I thought there was probably someone else in the group who would need protection as she opened herself to the transforming power of the Goddess.

One by one, we placed our gifts on the floor of the cave beside the rock. Each woman explained why she had chosen her gift. Everyone else probably wondered, as I did, which of the gifts, that included a silver Snake Goddess pendant, several small pithos jars, a tiny seal stone, a bag of seeds, one of Patricia's handmade Goddess statues, and a silver spiral, would be hers. Someone suggested that we each approach the altar, and with closed eyes, choose a gift. Jana got the shiny pink and blue abstract ceramic Goddess that Patricia, who is an artist, had made. Patricia went next. She was given Jana's small pithos jar. They felt that this coincidence was an affirmation of their developing friendship and their vow to come back to Crete together. When my turn came, I looked at all the beautiful gifts, my eyes focusing on the sealstone and the silver Snake Goddess. I closed my eyes and opened my hands, sensing the energy in various places on the altar. Disoriented, I reached down. I was pleased that I received the sealstone. Later, when I looked at it carefully, I saw that etched on its surface was of a couple in the act of intercourse. I laughed, hoping it was an omen. I could definitely use some of that in my life!

Gifts given and received, we began our goodbye ritual. Carol wove us together with red yarn. When she finished, we repeated, "We say goodbye," and each woman broke the cord that had bound her to the others. We did not want our time together to end, but the guard was restless. So we grounded the energy in the rocks of the cave and took our things from the altar.

"Don't leave anything in the cave," the guard called out, as several of us were climbing up to wedge our votive offerings into the crevices in the walls of the cave. "Don't worry, we won't," I called back, as I took my ceramic pitcher from the altar. Jana was near me as I claimed the two pairs of beads I had bought in the morning. "If you want," I said to her, "these beads can symbolize a sister-bonding ritual. We can tie them together like Naomi and I did, and leave them on Mount Ida." "I'd like that," Jana replied.

On the way down the hill, some of us tied our red yarn to to the leafless branches of a tree. It looked radiant with its red cords blowing in the wind. Others took theirs home to put on their altars. Just as we reached the plain, we passed through a flock of sheep.

MOUNTAIN WOMEN

*W*hen we arrived in Anogeia, Aristeia, the owner of the pension where we would spend the night, and her sister Constantina were waiting for us. Captivated by their vivacity and strength when I met them in the spring, I had asked Aristeia if they would be willing to share their stories with us. "Why are you so late?" Constantina began, as soon as I got off the bus. "I'm sick and I should be in bed. I'm here only as a favor to you." I hadn't expected them to be waiting, but I hastily apologized. "We'll start as soon as the group puts their bags in their rooms," I promised.

As soon as six or seven of us were seated in chairs on Aristeia's front porch, Constantina, a small, round, white-haired woman in her seventies, began speaking rapidly in Cretan dialect, her short arms flailing, her legs swinging back and forth not quite touching the ground. Our evening of sharing stories began with a free-for-all, as I tried to stop Constantina long enough to translate, or shouted the translation in English as she shouted on in Greek. Sometimes I had to ask Giannis to translate her rapid Cretan into Greek so I could translate it into English. Noticing the rapport between Giannis and me, Constantina interrupted her story briefly. She gestured with her two hands and asked him in Cretan if he was "banging" me. "Absolutely not," he replied. "For Karolina, I have the greatest respect." Satisfied, she continued her story.

Constantina's story was a hair-raising one, not requiring at all the high drama she had managed create around herself. She is thirteen years older than her baby sister Aristeia. Aristeia went to school, but when Constantina was little, they told her the teacher hit the children, and she would be better off in the mountains with the sheep and goats. She married during the war—by proxeniá, arranged marriage. She made it clear that she had not been in love with her husband. And sex? "Once a year is enough for me," she said slapping her hand against her fist.

When the Germans evacuated Anogeia in reprisal for resistance activity, she was eight months pregnant with her first child. With three hundred other pregnant women, she was marched down the mountains to another village where they were held in captivity. One night a voice called out to her. A friend of a relative had come to rescue her. Lots of wine was given to the German guards, who got drunk and passed out. Constantina and her savior escaped through the mountains. When they got to Anogeia, they saw that it had been burned to the ground. Constantina wanted to go to her house to see if she could salvage any-thing. But a German soldier who knew her, stopped her and told her that any Greeks found in the village would be shot. They continued through the mountains, stopping at the villages to ask if anyone had word of her husband who had been in the mountains with his sheep. At the third village, men were in the streets playing the lyre and singing. She said, "Have you no shame? Don't you know that Anogeia has been burned?" They responded, "Yes, we know. That is why we are singing. What else can we do?" In that village or the next one, she got news of her husband. He was safe. "Of course it was difficult after the war," she continued. "We had nothing. Most of our young men had been killed."

There was a lull in the conversation, and Aristeia, a strong woman with steely grey brillo-like hair pulled back in a tight bun, stepped in. "I am so glad you all are here," she began. "I was so happy to meet Karolina in the spring. Life in the villages is very hard for women. I think all women should be feminists. If we ran the world, things would be different. We need to get more women into government. I'd like to know what all of you are doing."

So we went around the circle, each of us sharing a little about her-self. Many of the women in the group were married and feminists. This surprised Constantina. But not as much as the response Robin gave her when she asked her if she had a boyfriend. "I don't think she wants one," the young Greek schoolteacher who had joined us, translated diplomatically. "Why not?" Constantina insisted. She got her answer. I don't think Constantina had ever heard the word "lesbian." "Two women together?" she kept repeating. "Why not?" Aristeia responded. Constantina shook her head, trying to fit one open hand into the other, struggling to comprehend the information she had just been given. As we continued around the circle, Aristeia repeated, "Good! Good!" And, "Bravo! Bravo!" She told us that her husband had been sick for many years before he died. "I started with rooms-to-rent, and built this hotel with the money I made and a loan from the bank. My daughters said, 'Why don't you name the hotel after yourself. You did all the work.' So I did."

Experience had made Aristeia and Constantina hard as rock. Like Mount Ida they would endure. They were images of the Goddess we sought, reflecting the strength we were discovering within ourselves.

MINOAN SISTERHOOD

$\int$ ince our ritual at Zakros, Jana, Robin, Patricia, Cathleen, and I had unconsciously gravitated together. On our last afternoon in Heraklion, a number of us left the museum together to go for lunch. By the time we found the restaurant Patricia had chosen, we were only five. Some went back to buy postcards at the museum, others stopped to shop, and two decided to try another restaurant. After we had ordered, Robin said, "Do you realize that we five are together again? I think it is significant that we seem so drawn to each other." We looked around the table. On the surface, we were an unlikely combination. Cathleen and Robin sometimes got on each other's nerves. Though we would always think of her wearing bermuda shorts and athletic shoes, it was easy to imagine Patricia, in other clothes, attending parties in Washington society with her husband. Cathleen was earthy and working class. Robin, a free spirit. Jana lived a quiet life in rural Virginia. I, an exotic one in Athens. But something *had* drawn us together.

We began talking about the Zakros initiation and its power. We each knew that something very important had happened, but none of us was yet able articulate its meaning. The Goddess had not appeared in the midst of our dance, but we sensed that She had drawn us together and guided our steps. "We must keep in touch by letter," we agreed, "so that we remember. When we leave Crete and each other, it will be easy to forget what happened."

Someone suggested that we spend the rest of the afternoon shopping for a symbol we could each take home with us, to remind us of the mystery we had shared and had yet to unravel. We decided that though we would talk to others about the experience as Zakros, the symbol we would find to commemorate it would remain our secret. It took us most of the afternoon to find the right symbol, but when we did, we knew immediately that it was right.

We just had time to get back to the hotel to pick up our bags and meet the bus that would take the group to the ferryboat. Though I was going to Maria and Giorgios' for dinner and flying out later in evening, I decided to go with the group to the boat. I didn't want to part from them.

On the bus, Giannis gave me a large round cookie tin filled with the tiny Cretan olives he knew I loved. "When you do the trip again in the spring, please ask for me as a driver," he requested. "Of course I will," I replied. Since I was the only one who could speak Greek, Giannis and I had shared many meals and much laughter together, even discovering one night that we have the same birthday. Our travel agent Rena had warned me that the busdriver could make or break the trip. Among our many blessings, I counted Giannis.

When we arrived at the dock, the group collected their bags and began ascending the steep stairs of the ferryboat. I watched until they were all inside, knowing that, though I would see them all the next day in Athens, this was the end of our pilgrimage.

Part Four

REVELATIONS

Snake Goddesses from Knossos in Minoan ritual costume

I approached the very gates of death and set foot on Proserpine's threshhold, yet was permitted to return, rapt through all the elements. At midnight I saw the sun shining as if it were noon. I entered the presence of the Goddesses and Gods of the underworld and of the upper-world, stood near and worshiped them.

· Apuleius

~∿ When I returned from Crete, my continuing illness gave me time to incubate the knowledge that I had gained. I had learned that the Goddess had not ever abandoned me. I had felt Her presence throughout the odyssey of the previous year. My experiences in Crete had confirmed that love and help are present at every turn in the path of life. My initiation at Zakros had given me symbols that would guide my journey.

I was finally ready to incorporate the mystery revealed to me as my mother died into my life. But first I had to uproot the competing belief embedded in the phrase: "No one loves me." Sick and tired from the effort to keep those words from destroying me, I drifted back to the place of their origin and discovered the root of my despair in my father's command to control myself. My father's words were the legacy of a culture (his father was German, his mother Irish, his grandparents immigrants, his birthplace New York) that valued discipline, control, and achievement above all. Ultimately his words were the reflection of a judgmental Father God whose perfection, it is said, is that he is unaffected and unmoved by his creation.

Though I had long understood the Goddess to be the embodiment of life and change, the power that supports relational being, I was still living my life under the sway of the fathers and the Father. I believed I was essentially alone, and I feared that if I let go of whatever tenuous control I had over my life, I would die.

Once I understood the origin of my despair, the words "No one loves me" lost their power over me. I could stop trying so hard to stay in control and allow myself to feel. It sounds so simple. But for me it was not. It took me many years to unlearn the lesson I had learned so well as a child.

Since my return from Crete, I feel that a veil has been lifted from before my eyes. I see the love that surrounds me—in the bounteous earth and in the faces of others—more clearly and feel it more deeply. This does not mean I am always happy or that I never experience pain. But now that I am not so desperate for love, I can recognize other people's limitations and inability to love without feeling that some lack in me caused their behavior. I can let my feelings ebb and flow like the currents of the sea, no longer trying to control myself or anyone else. As I move forward and back along the serpentine path of my life, I know that I am not alone and never have been.

INCUBATION

$\mathcal{A}$fter I said good-bye to the group in Athens, I collapsed. For several weeks, I spent most of every day in bed, watching television and sleeping, coughing whenever I tried to talk. Though I was sick, I didn't feel sad or depressed. The trip had gone better than I had ever dared hope. But I was too tired to think much about how I felt. I knew only that I needed rest. And I gave myself permission to take it. I didn't have much choice. It was a struggle to drag myself out of bed, and talking on the phone brought on coughing fits.

Much of those two weeks feel hazy as I try to remember them. I must have been in the midst of the "breakdown" I had told Jana I feared. As my therapist Charis Katakis describes it, this breakdown happens when the fixed beliefs that have guided your life no longer function. With no new beliefs to organize reality, you feel at a loss, adrift, unsure of yourself and others.[1] Melpo had been feeling this way for some weeks. I was beginning to feel it too. As we had done throughout the fall and summer, Melpo and I spoke several times each day, reassuring each other and sharing our feelings.

I got out of bed after six days to go to therapy. Charis was not there. Patrick smiled encouragingly as I began to speak. "The tour went really well," I began. "Everyone loved it. The only problem was that I was tired during the whole trip, and I am exhausted now. I couldn't stop crying after therapy three weeks ago, and because of that, I missed my plane. I was afraid I wouldn't be able to regain control, so that I could lead the group. I'm afraid of losing control, because I feel that I have two personalities. The one that is sad, is so sad that she wants to commit suicide. I am afraid of her."

"The timing may have been bad," Patrick said, removing his glasses and looking directly at me, "but I'm glad you lost control. You may be scared, but I like the person who is here in the room with us now. She is not trying so hard. She feels softer and less driven than the other Karolina. She is human and vulnerable. I think she is the 'real' you. Everybody likes her." He hesitated, put his glasses back on, and smiled shyly, clearly aware that I was skeptical. "Everyone likes her," he repeated with great gentleness. "Look around and see." I looked around the circle of women and saw that everyone was smiling at me. "I want to hug you," one of the women said, getting up and crossing the room to put her arms around me.

I wasn't sure what to make of Patrick's words, but I took comfort in his calm, accepting manner. "It didn't really matter to the others that I was tired on the trip," I continued. "No one expected me to be in control of everything. The group seemed to enjoy reading together from the guidebook. And people kept appearing to help me, even when I didn't think I needed help. I had told the man who guides people into the Skoteino cave that we wanted to be alone. But when he turned up, I had to accept his help. And it was so much easier to let him show us the way. Things like that kept happening throughout the trip. I didn't have to do everything all by myself." Patrick nodded.

When I got home, I went back to bed, but I wasn't afraid any more. Something was changing inside me. I felt like a bear in hibernation or a butterfly in a cocoon. Gradually, over the next weeks, I came to understand that the timing of my breakdown was exactly right. I remembered reading that in many traditions the person who is called to become a shaman or priestess becomes ill before receiving initiation. The stronger the person is, the harder it is to let go, to admit that there is more to be learned. My control was so strong, it had to be taken from me.

INSIGHT

"It sounds to me like you are 'sick and tired,'" Rena said when she called to ask how the trip had gone. "'Sick and tired' of it all,'" she repeated definitively. Her words made me wonder what it was that had made me so sick and so tired. Gradually it dawned on me that I was sick and tired of the constant struggle to stay in control. As I lay in my bed, drifting in and out of sleep, I remembered that one of the things my dad often said to me in my childhood was: "Control yourself." He would say it when I was crying and feeling sorry for myself, when I was angry, and even when my mom and my brother and I were laughing and giggling when we were happy. It wasn't only sadness and anger that I was told I had to control, but also joy.

I recalled that one of the times my dad told me to "control myself" was when my mother and my baby brother Brian came home from the hospital. I was just over two and a half years old. I was in the front seat of the car with my dad. I kept jumping up and turning around to see my mom and the new baby. My dad said, "Control yourself. You're a big girl now."

I had often thought that my brother's birth must have been traumatic for me. I imagined that I must have been insanely jealous when I thought of my later animosity toward my brother. Now I remembered that I had been excited by my brother's birth. Perhaps I had also been jealous. But jealousy of a new baby is natural. I needed to be reassured that I was still loved. But my mother was busy with the new baby, and my father did not tell me what I needed to hear. In my two-and-a-half-year-old's mind, I must have felt that the only way I could retain my parents' love was by "controlling myself," and "becoming a big girl." It was too hard. I was only a little girl. But I tried. And I had been trying ever since.

I understood that the voice that says, "*No one understands me, no one loves me, maybe I should just die*" was born of my struggle to suppress my feelings, to grow up, to control myself. Little Carol had never really wanted to die. All she had ever wanted was love. What she really wanted to say was: "*I hurt, I want, I feel, I am.*"

Now when I hear the words, "*No one understands me, no one loves me, I want to die,*" echoing in my mind—and I will hear them again, from time to time—I will not be so afraid. I will feel sympathy for little Carol and for big Carol, for whom the struggle to stay in control was just too difficult. I will replace the refrain of ancient pain with the words I have learned they masked: *I hurt, I want, I feel, I am.* If those were the words hidden under the familiar litany that so frightened me, there was, in fact, nothing to be afraid of. The darkness inside that I had feared was human feeling. Like the darkness in the cave, it was a place of transformation.

A SERPENTINE PATH

In the next days, I rested and my cough started to get better. I felt soft and open, vulnerable as a newborn baby. I spoke often with Melpo, and I received letters and beautiful photographs from Jana and Patricia. As I began my addition to the "round robin" letter we had promised to write, memories of Zakros became vivid. As I thought of the snakelike path I had traced on the ancient stones, my eyes fixed on the gold snake bracelet on my right arm. I thought of the many meanings the snake held for me. Goddess temples were centers of grain storage, the harvest returned to She who gave it; snakes were guardians of the temples, protecting the grain from mice and rats. The coiled snake and the snake biting its tail are symbols of wholeness. Snakes shed their skin and are symbols of rebirth or immortality. Snakes go under the Earth and above the Earth, connecting the underworld and the upper world. But there was something more: the rhythm of the snake in movement. I picked up my pen and wrote the phrase: "*the serpentine path.*"

Those were the words I had been searching for as I sought to name the experience of Zakros! The serpentine path was the path of my life, a snakelike, meandering path, winding in and out, up and down. The antithesis of the "straight and narrow." A path that does not ever "come to a point." Two steps left, two steps right. Into the darkness, into the light. Not the goal, but the journey.

I sensed a cycle coming to completion. The rebirth of spring and the intense work of summer completed in the fall harvest. Through my odyssey in Crete, I had found my way back to the Goddess, and to myself. I had integrated the mystery that was revealed to me as my mother died. I was not alone. Love had never abandoned me and never would. I did not have to try to control my life. I could simply experience my feelings, relax, and live.

And I wanted to live! I had begun to trust my deepest intuitions again, but not blindly as before. My muse had returned. Words were flowing out of me, the more poetic words I came to Greece to write. I would return again and again to the mountains and caves of Crete, by myself, with friends, and with other pilgrims. My life would be filled with amazing grace, love abounding and overflowing.

I lit the candles on my altar, called the names Skoteiní, Vritomartis, Aphrodite, Panagia Myrtiá, Panagia Paliani. I thanked the Goddesses and asked them to guide me as I found my way. I did not know who or what might lie ahead on the serpentine path, but I felt the same sense of eagerness and anticipation I had experienced at Zakros. The dance is about to begin. The dance of my life. It begins anew every day.

Two steps forward
One step back
Into the darkness
Into the light

Women dancing in a circle to the music of a lyre player

Tell everyone

*Now, today, I shall
sing beautifully for
my friends' pleasure*

· Sappho

NOTES

• UNDERWORLD •

The quote that begins this section is taken from Homer, *The Odyssey, Book XI*, Walter Shewring, trans. (Oxford: Oxford University Press, 1980), 128.

1. *Sappho: A New Translation,* Mary Barnard, trans. (Berkeley: University of California Press, 1958), no. 63. "Cyprian" is an epithet for Aphrodite, who was said to have come ashore at Paphos on the island of Cyprus.

2. Not all archaeologists identify the temple as Aphrodite's. Vincent Scully convincingly argues that the temple's location embodies Aphrodite in "the stretched-out fullness of land and water, marsh, mountain, and sea, perfectly shaped, engrossing and complete." See *The Earth, the Temple, and the Gods: Greek Sacred Architecture*, rev. ed. (New Haven: Yale University Press 1979), 219.

3. Here and elsewhere in this book, I write of hearing the Goddess. In other cultures, such experiences are an ordinary and accepted part the spiritual path. In our rational culture, they are questioned. For me this "hearing," which has occurred only a few times in my life, happens when I am in an agitated state and have spoken all the words in my heart. The words come into my mind, but they do not seem to me to be my words, or even to come from an unconscious, deeper, or split-off part of my self. Rather, they feel like a gift from a source outside myself, and I choose to interpret them as such. Of course, there is no proof that this is the case. The Roman Catholic mystical tradition has a practice called testing visions and voices. While I do not submit my voices to the "authority of the church," I have learned that it is a good idea to test my voices. When what I "hear" sounds like what I want, I am suspicious and withhold judgment. I would not follow a voice that told me to do something I knew was wrong.

4. I have written more fully about this experience in my book *Laughter of Aphrodite: Reflections on a Journey to the Goddess* (San Francisco: Harper & Row, 1987), 87–192.

5. See Jane Ellen Harrison, *Prolegomena to the Study of Greek Religion* (London: Merlin Press, 1962), 285. The quote refers to Hesiod, but Harrison makes similar criticisms of Homer.

6. See *Laughter of Aphrodite*, 92–199.

7. See "Reflections on the Initiation of an American Woman Scholar into the Symbols and Rituals of the Ancient Goddesses," published with companion pieces by Karen McCarthy Brown and Rita M. Gross in *Journal of Feminist Studies in Religion* 3, no. 1 (1987), and in different form in *Laughter of Aphrodite*, 182–205.

8. See my *Diving Deep and Surfacing: Women Writers on Spiritual Quest*, 2d ed. (Boston: Beacon Press, 1986).

9. Though her doctors denied that the estrogen my mother was given as an antidote to osteoperosis caused her cancer, I believe, and I think my mother came to believe, that she was poisoned by her doctors. My mother was also severely burned by her radiologist. With uncharacteristic bitterness, she called him "a butcher."

10. See Harrison, *Prolegomena to the Study of Greek Religion*, 274.

11. Notice the recurrence of this theme in my own life, in my inability to accept help, a pattern that begins to be tranformed in Part 3, "Pilgrimage."

12. My mother and her sister had a powerful psychic connection. They each conceived four children at about the same time. I was born three months after my cousin Dee, and my brothers were born within two weeks of two other cousins. My mother had a late miscarriage that would have resulted in a baby the same age as her sister's third child. My mother's sister also died of cancer shortly after her seventy-second birthday. Perhaps thinking of my mother's torture by her doctors, my aunt refused all treatment and had a better quality of life in her last months than my mother.

13. This image resonates with the "life after life" experiences described by Elizabeth Kübler-Ross and others. I neither believed nor disbelieved the accounts of being met by loved ones at the hour of death before my mother died. These experiences do not, as it is sometimes suggested they do, verify the Christian notion of "eternal life" after death. If true, they tell us something about the moment of death, but not about what comes after that. These experiences of death are equally compatible with the notion that life after death is conditional, dependent, for example, on the memories of the living. See my *Thealogy*, forthcoming, for a fuller discussion of my understanding of life after death.

14. I Corinthians 13: 1–8a, 13, from the Revised Standard Version of the Bible; "tongues of men" changed to "tongues of humans." The RSV does not print this passage as poetry. Many scholars believe that this poem, though found in the letters of Paul, is not original to Paul, but was a Hellenistic hymn or poem that Paul adopted or adapted into his text. I read this poem as part of the eulogy at my mother's funeral.

15. I have come to believe that the knowledge gained at the moment of death is the "mystery" that was revealed at Eleusis.

16. See "Learning from My Mother Dying," in Christine Downing, *The Long Journey Home: Revisioning the Myth of Demeter and Persephone for Our Time* (Boston: Shambala Press, 1994), 125–139. A somewhat different version of that essay became the chapter entitled "Death" in this book.

· REBIRTH ·

The poem that begins this section is from *Sappho: A New Translation*, Mary Barnard, trans. (Berkeley: University of California Press, 1958), no. 84.

1. See Bogdan Rutkowski, *The Cult Places of the Aegean* (New Haven: Yale University Press, 1987), 51.

2. Many archaeologists believe that Skoteinó was the sacred cave of Knossos. See, e.g., Stylianos Alexiou, *Minoan Civilization*, 3d rev. ed., Cressida Ridley, trans. (Spyros Alexiou Sons: Heraclion, Crete, n.d.), 80. The Homeric hymn "To Demeter" states that the Eleusinian mysteries were brought from Crete. Archaeologists at Eleusis have looked in vain for a subterranean cave or chamber. Perhaps the original cave was in Crete.

3. Robert Bly is an American poet who runs workshops aimed at putting men in touch with the elemental masculine. However, his workshops direct a great deal of venom against the mother and against feminism. In contrast, the "men's mysteries" in Crete express a longing for reunion with the female.

4. It is said that the Dionysian festival which was the origin of Greek tragedy, was originally a goat dance, which is to say that it was rooted in the singing and dancing of shepherds. Tina Salowey showed me a striking parallel between at least one of the rakí songs and the "bucolic poems" of Theokritos, the fourth century B.C.E. poet. Theokritos, self-consciously reproducing shepherds' traditions, wrote the following lines about the lovesick Polyphemus: "Often enough his sheep had to find their own way home / to the field from green pastures, while he sang of Galetea." Another line says, "You'd surely show more sense if you keep at your basket weaving [weave baskets to set cheese] / and go gather olive shoots and give them to the lambs. / Milk the ewe that's at hand." See *The Poems of Theocrites*, trans. and intro, Anna Rist (Chapel Hill: University of North Carolina Press, 1978), Idyll 11: 106, 108.

5. See Loweta Tyree, *Cretan Sacred Caves* (Ann Arbor: University Microfilms, 1975).

6. Although I did not think of it at the time, doves are sacred to Aphrodite. Later I read that Arthur Evans, the excavator of Knossos, believed that the Skoteinó cave was sacred to Aphrodite, though his evidence has been questioned. See Loweta Tyree, *Cretan Sacred Caves*, 109.

7. A friend once suggested to me that I have the psychology of a child of an alcoholic. It was then that I began to wonder if my grandfather was an alcoholic. My parents do not remember him that way, but my cousin confirmed my suspicion. Note that when I describe the ways that my father and I are alike in this paragraph, I miss the obvious: that I too felt I needed to be in control. My own need to control becomes one of the prominent themes of Part 3, "Pilgrimage," and Part 4, "Return."

8. George Sfikas, *Trees and Shrubs of Greece*, Ellen Sutton, trans. (Athens: Efstathiadis Group, 1978), 104.

9. Christine Downing, *Gods in Our Midst* (New York: Crossroad, 1993), 51–66.

10. Downing, 56.

· PILGRIMAGE ·

The poem that begins this section is from *Sappho: A New Translation*, Mary Barnard, trans. (Berkeley: University of California Press, 1958), no. 23.

1. See Lucy Goodison, *Moving Heaven and Earth: Sexuality, Spirituality, and Social Change* (London: The Women's Press, 1990), 68. Goodsion argues that the influence of the warlike Mycenean culture may have been felt in Crete as early as 1600 B.C.E.;

therefore she limits her discussion to the period before 1600 B.C.E. This distinction is lacking in other important books on ancient Crete, including those by Nanno Marinatos and Bogdan Rutkowski, cited here.

2. All references to Nanno Marinatos are taken from her *Minoan Religion: Ritual, Image, and Symbol* (Columbia: University of South Carolina Press, 1993). Marinatos proposes that the "temple complexes" were controlled by a "religious elite." I am not convinced by her evidence.

3. Jacquetta Hawkes, *Dawn of the Gods* (London: Sphere Books, 1972).

4. I have discussed this point in *Laughter of Aphrodite*, 161–180.

5. The guidebooks referred to unclude J. A. Sakellarokis, *Heraklion Museum: Illustrated Guide to the Museum*, Sylvia Moody, trans. (Athens: Ekdotike Athenon, S. A., 1987); Anna Kofou, *Crete: All the Museums and Archeological Sites*, 2nd. ed., Phillip Ramp, trans. (Athens: Ekdotike Athenon, S. A., 1990); and Pat Cameron *Blue Guide Crete*, 6th ed. (New York: WW Norton & Company, 1993).

6. Marija Gimbutas, *The Language of the Goddess* (San Francisco: Harper & Row, 1989).

7. Vincent Scully convincingly argues that the Minoan "palaces" were deliberately situated within the surrounding landscape. See *The Earth, the Temple, and the Gods*, 11.

8. In the agrarian economy, cows and female sheep and goats are valued for their milk and their ability to reproduce. Only a few males are needed to mate with a large number of females. The others are killed for their meat. In rural Greece, the "paschal lamb" is no symbol. Hundreds of sheep and goats, most of them male, are slaughtered on Easter weekend. The custom of ritual animal sacrifice arises from (but is not fully explained by) the practices of agricultural life. The male animals do not produce milk, and if they were all allowed to survive, they would diminish or deplete the supply of greens and grasses eaten by the females and their young.

9. Gimbutas, *The Language of the Goddess*, 26–7.

10. See Jeremiah 44:19.

11. Ellen Boneparth noted that the cough that characterized my initiatory illness paralleled the cough that was the first sign of my mother's cancer. In psychological terms, a cough indicates that one has "swallowed" harmful words or "swallowed" feelings.

12. Cathleen Hope Peterson, used by permission.

13. *Sappho*, Mary Barnard, trans. Poem no. 37; the second line reads "Leave Crete and come to us," reflecting Sappho's location in Lesbos. For the poems that follow, see Nos. 16, 6, 98, 29.

14. See *Moving Heaven and Earth*, 74–77.

15. See Athanasia Kanta, "Minoan and Traditional Crete: Some Parallels between Two Cultures in the Same Environment," in *Minoan Society: Proceedings of the Cambridge Colloquim 1981*, Olga Krzyszkowska and Lucia Nixon, eds. (Bristol Classics Press, 1983), 155–162.

· RETURN ·

The quote that begins this section is from Apuleius, *Transformations of Lucius Otherwise Known as the Golden Ass*, Robert Graves, trans. (New York: Farrar, Straus & Giroux, 1951), 280, "gods of the underworld and gods of the upper-world" changed to

"Goddesses and Gods of the underworld and of the upper-world." The poem that ends this section is from *Sappho: A New Translation*, Mary Barnard, trans. (Berkeley: University of California Press, 1958), no. 1.

1. Charis Katakis, "Stages of Psychotherapy: Progressive Reconceptualizations as a Self-Organizing Process," *Psychotherapy, Theory, Research, Practice and Training* 26 (1989), 484–93.

GODDESS PILGRIMAGE TOURS

For further information about Goddess Pilgrimage Tours to Crete led by Carol P. Christ, write or call:

> The Continuum Publishing Group
> 370 Lexington Avenue
> New York, NY 10017
>
> Phone: 212/953-5858
> Fax: 212/953-5944